MW00422747

"As a Christian counselor, the two biggest barriers I see holding God's children in bondage are unforgiveness and negative thinking. Juda Myers' insight and anointing truly shed light on the power of our thoughts and the blessings we receive when we choose to practice forgiveness. It's never too late to apply these life giving, practical steps, the principles of His word, to attain true forgiveness and right thinking in Christ."

Marie Denton,
Christian Counselor
Humble, Texas

"*Hostile Conception Living with Purpose.* A must read for inspiration from real-life stories and actual methods of implementing forgiveness, proving God gives life and purpose to all He creates."

Nina Ward,
Cup of Grace Coffeehouse
Ministry Director and Author
Humble, Texas

"Words carry power. Positive and negative power. From the moment you open Hostile Conception, you will feel the power of each word as it pulsates from the page and draws tears from a place deep within. This is a book you will find very hard to put down. This book speaks of a victim's journey to becoming a victor. In each of our lives we can relate to a victim's struggle, but as you read Hostile Conception, the light of the love of Jesus will shine through and resonate in your heart, shining on the overcomer."

Dr. Jacquelyn Hadnot Author & Psalmist
Glori Radio www.gloriradio.com
www.jacquiehadnot.com

HOSTILE CONCEPTION

Living With Purpose

JUDA MYERS

HOSTILE
CONCEPTION

Living With Purpose

TATE PUBLISHING & Enterprises

Hostile Conception Living With Purpose!
Copyright © 2009 by Juda Myers. All rights reserved.

No part of this publication may be reproduced, stored in a retrieval system or transmitted in any way by any means, electronic, mechanical, photocopy, recording or otherwise without the prior permission of the author except as provided by USA copyright law.

Scripture quotations marked "NIV" are taken from the *Holy Bible, New International Version* ®, Copyright © 1973, 1978, 1984 by International Bible Society. Used by permission of Zondervan Publishing House. All rights reserved.

The opinions expressed by the author are not necessarily those of Tate Publishing, LLC.

Published by Tate Publishing & Enterprises, LLC
127 E. Trade Center Terrace | Mustang, Oklahoma 73064 USA
1.888.361.9473 | www.tatepublishing.com

Tate Publishing is committed to excellence in the publishing industry. The company reflects the philosophy established by the founders, based on Psalm 68:11,
"The Lord gave the word and great was the company of those who published it."

Book design copyright © 2009 by Tate Publishing, LLC. All rights reserved.
Cover design by Kandi Evans
Interior design by Travis Kimble

Published in the United States of America

ISBN: 978–1–60696–013–4
1. Self-Help: Motivational & Inspirational
2. Biography & Autobiography: Personal Memoirs
08.12.30

To Ann Phillips, who chose to make a right out of a wrong by giving life to me. She became my hero in doing so. To Edward and Alma McMillan, Daddy and Mama, for loving me as their own. To Matilda Gradneigo, who also loved me as her own, showing unconditional love. To all those people who have touched my life in good ways or bad to make me the person I am today. Most importantly to God who gives life and purpose to all He creates.

TABLE OF CONTENTS

Foreword

We are so fast to hit the delete button or remove what we do not understand before we see the big picture. We are at the beginning of the end times where God is taking the foolish things of the world and confusing the wise. Through our eyes we see God allowed such a horrific act to take place. But this eight-man rape allowed him to produce such a perfect product of himself.

We all are products of God made up of purpose, pace and process. Purpose: our life is predestined before we are even born. Pace: how long it takes us in life to realize what our purpose is. And then the process, which consists of death, burial, and resurrection. Our old negative way of thinking is dead, so we bury it, and a new positive God-centered way of thinking is resurrected. When this takes place in our life, we become active products of God. He can then see himself in us and begin to use us to impact others in a positive way.

I thank Ann Phillips for seeing the light and listening to that small, still voice not to hit the delete button of life through abortion. She sacrificed nine months with even more pain of carrying the unknown. What an act of forgiveness, not just to man but to God.

We are in the year 2008, where it's okay and more common than ever to hit the delete button of life—abortion. If the enemy had succeeded with Ann Phillips, then God's plan would have been hindered. The enemy is such a liar. He would have you to think that the product of God that was carried as the unknown would amount to nothing, so much that the enemy himself would do his best to hinder the blessing of God by lying and afflicting pain and hurt with statements like, "You are worthless," "God had nothing to do with your existence," and "You think God loves you." But there is a big God with a master plan.

I'm so glad that God chose me to be affected by such a powerful product of him, who has become a lifetime friend not just to me but my family as well. We love you, Juda Myers, and thank you for not listening to statements of the enemy. Thank you for documenting the struggle and hurt that was afflicted upon you. Just to endure, press on, and then write about it to help others, we witness an act of forgiveness and love.

The enemy would have you to think, "You are nothing," "No one is in your corner," "There's no light at the end of the tunnel," and most of all, "You have no value." It's lies! The enemy's job is to convince you to push the delete button of life, be it your own life or your unborn baby. After reading this book I pray that you, the reader, will find the path that will help you step into your freedom from bondage, because God has a master plan for your life. Don't give up—there is always hope.

Pastor Ben D. Richardson II
Author, Life before Adam

INTRODUCTION

Life begins at the moment of conception. Science has proven that at that exact moment, DNA is complete to create a human being. How a life is conceived is not as important as the life itself. People have searched for the meaning of life for centuries. Having been conceived in a most horrible way and having lived *full* of life, I hope to offer others the freedom I have found through forgiveness. We are faced with choices each and every moment. Life is ongoing choices. If we make the right choices, our life will be better for it. We cannot escape pain, but misery truly is a choice.

That still small voice that leads us to right actions must be allowed to speak often. We must be able to hear it and move forward. I hope that God's voice will speak as you read through these chapters. My prayer is that you will grasp the opportunity to know God's love for yourself through forgiveness, both from God and through God to forgive others. Knowing the value of life will bring great meaning to life. Knowing the creator of life will bring purpose to life.

I pray that you will rethink your thinking. Within these chapters are inspiration and actual methods of implementing forgiveness. Continued actions form habits. Don't ever give up. Difficulties don't mean failure. Failures don't mean worthlessness. Worthlessness does not mean one is unredeemable. There is always hope. Always. The value of life was proven when Jesus Christ showed we were worth the cost of *His* life. You alone can choose to agree for a life with unsurpassable meaning and untouchable freedom.

Ann (Juda's birthmother) and Juda (Dec. 2005)

Juda's adopted mom (1941)

Juda as a baby with her adopted dad (1958)

Juda's adopted dad,
in uniform (1942)

Juda's adopted dad (2006)

SEEING THE LIGHT

"I told you, you are worthless!" came the voice from behind. "God had nothing to do with your existence," another pounded from the left. Still another mocked, "And you think God loves you?"

Staring at nothing I could identify, through the blur of tears, I just sat there. I can't remember if I even made a sound as my spirit was beaten almost to death by each word. I had fought so hard against these voices before, and I had won. Over and over, they tried their best to convince me I was useless and unloved. I had pressed forward dragging them behind me.

Struggles to have purpose and value always left me feeling I was pretending. Relationships suffered, never fulfilling my need to be loved. Even after accepting Jesus Christ in 1986, the voices would come to take me away from the security of His love. I managed with the strength of God alone to battle these forces. Somehow each time I managed to overcome. But now these voices seemed to have the ammunition for the final blow that would surely end it all.

My mind struggled with what I knew before and what I knew right then.

Think! Think! My mother had sacrificed nine months to give me life, and Jesus Christ died so I could live. *Come on, think!* I had made a conscious decision twenty-six years earlier to give my life to Christ. Not one day had I ever regretted that decision. This day Jesus was my *only* reason to live.

Words are powerful. With all the power of hell, the words cut to my deepest core. "You're worthless. You have the blood of a rapist running through your veins." The words pierced my heart. "Oh God!" my insides cried as I could literally feel what seemed like demons pulsating through every vessel in my body. More forcefully the voice said, "The only thing you can do is slash your wrists and let all that nasty blood flow out. No one will miss you."

The pain was more that I could have ever imagined. I couldn't get away. Then I heard my own voice saying, "My life doesn't belong to me. It belongs to Jesus, and I cannot take my life."

The demonic pulsation stopped. Only a couple of minutes had passed, but I was exhausted. "I may not be able to live, but I cannot kill myself," I whispered.

———

Life appears to be like a roller coaster sometimes. This same day had started out almost miraculously. Only two hours earlier I had kissed my husband good-bye, insisting he stay at the airport in Lafayette, Louisiana, while I went off to retrieve the information about my birthmother. We were so happy, finally getting the missing pieces of my life puzzle.

This day had begun with our flying into Alexandria, Louisiana. I left Richard at the airport, and I drove a rental car to the courthouse there in Alexandria. This had been the first step in getting the release of my birth records. I later had to go to Lafayette to get information from the adoption agency where I was adopted. Alexandria held legal records, and Lafayette held personal records about my birthmother. The way things happened seemed to be divinely planned.

I entered the courthouse early and found no one in the office. There was a nice man waiting for the elevator with his shirt out of his pants and his tie hanging around his shoulders. He looked like he was still getting dressed. I asked him if I was in the right place. He said, "Sure, just go through the door with the sign saying 'Employees only'!"

Okay then, I thought and thanked the man. This was kind of strange, but the man was right. I was in the correct place. The woman was expecting me and greeted me with excitement. The woman then went to a different office and returned with the documents in a folder. She handed it to me and told me the battle was still not over. The next step was to convince a judge to sign the paperwork.

Judges were on the fifth floor, and I was standing on the first. It was the longest elevator ride ever. Not only could I hear my heart pounding, I think I saw it pounding too.

The doors of the elevator opened up right into the reception area. The receptionist told me that the regular judge wasn't there, but there was a substitute on duty. She said I should have a seat and wait. Thoughts raced through my mind: *What is going to happen? Did God get me this far to not have my records? Oh please, God, let the judge sign the papers.*

The man I had spoken with near the elevators earlier

interrupted my thoughts. "Hey, what are you doing here?" he asked.

I began telling him and then interrupted myself to ask, "Do you have any pull with the judge?" I needed all the help I could get.

Just at that time another man walked off the elevator and shouted, "Hey, judge!"

"What? You're a *judge?*" I said with fright and excitement.

"Oh no, they just call me that," he said. "I'll see what I can do." He smiled and disappeared with the other man down the hall.

Moments later the other man came out and said to me, "Judge will see you now."

I walked down the hall slowly and saw an open door. As I walked in I couldn't see his desk because it was behind the door. I peeked around the door, and who did I see but the man who told me he *wasn't* a judge. It was the same man I had met at the elevators with his shirt out of his pants but was now fully dressed.

"Please don't do this to me. I can't take it. *Are you a judge or not?*" I was crying by now, an emotional roller wreck.

This sweet man came out from behind his desk and gave me the biggest hug. As I looked up I noticed a Christian plaque above his door. I was so happy asking, "So, you're a Christian?" *Oh, thank you, Lord, thank*—I stopped right there and in shock looked at him and asked, "So are you going to sign my—" Before I could say paper, he was signing it looking up at me with a big smile. I believe God had put this man there this day just to sign my papers.

"I don't get to do this kind of thing often. People aren't usually happy with me. I'm glad I could make someone smile," the judge admitted. Wow, I was on cloud, well, whichever one is the highest. I know it was way above ten!

So I had to go back downstairs and give the documents to the woman on the first floor. The elevator ride down was much better than going up. I shared my story with everyone as they stood amazed and happy for me. The same reaction continued as I told anyone that would listen.

The woman, who had searched for my birth records, shared the same joy everyone else did. She happily went to the back office to retrieve the info. Returning with a manila folder, she smiled and handed it to me. But I just stared at her, paralyzed, unable to open it.

"I can't do it," I said. I had never felt like this before. A mixture of feeling stupid and embarrassed I had felt before, but nothing like this.

This woman was sensitive and kind. She said she'd make copies of my records so I could open them later when I felt comfortable. It was such a relief, and I was so grateful for her insight.

The next step was to call the adoption agency where I had been adopted. I wanted to let them know I was on my way to get their information. I called while waiting for my copies right there in the courthouse. To my surprise, even after telling the agency's social worker I had a court order, she still said she'd have to talk to their lawyer. At first, she just said she wouldn't be able to give me that info. I told her I would be there with the court order in one hour. If she still refused, she would be in contempt of court.

Many people don't have these problems now. The adoption process today is much better, allowing openness with a lot of adoptions. Records are frequently available to everyone involved in the adoption. Biological mothers either keep in touch with the children or leave information and photos to be given to the child at the appropriate time. I would not have had to spend all the time and money if my adoption had been an open one. Wanting to know our heritage or where we came from seems to be a natural desire. I wanted to know my heritage also. My mirror kept me wondering who I looked like. Other adoptees wonder too. Something in us wants to know. That's why many people are into genealogies. A movie was made very popular because of that desire. It was called *Roots*. History is important for purpose in the present. God also kept a record of ancestry and it is listed in the bible. God gives us a longing to know our past. Maybe the longing to know our history is God wanting us to go even further to find our origins in Him.

Now, the court worker handed me my birth records. I thanked her, took the folder, and went to my rental car. Well, the first part of the adventure was done. I threw the folder on the seat and just sat there staring straight ahead. I looked down at the folder and thought of how silly I was being. Picking it up, I realized I had waited so long for this. It was a very emotional time for me, and I had no idea what I would find in those records, but

I *could* do this. Besides, no one was with me to see my reactions. I opened the folder skimming quickly to find *her* name. There was the name given to me at birth, Mary Elizabeth. For the first time, I saw another name attached to it—Hoover. *"Hoover? What?"* I had been told I was Irish all my life! Talk about identity crisis. I threw down the folder refusing to accept that name. Confused, I tried to regain my senses and picked up the folder once more. I stared at the name—Mary Elizabeth Hoover. Then I looked further down, and there it was—my mother's name. She suddenly became a real person to me. I really wanted to know more now, but I would have to get that from the adoption agency in Lafayette, Louisiana. I put the folder back down on the seat and drove back to the airport in Alexandria to pick up my husband.

I must have been on autopilot because to this day I don't remember the drive there. My husband, Richard, was waiting anxiously. He and I then drove to the airport in Lafayette, where he waited for me once again to retrieve my records, this time from the adoption agency. The agency was only five miles from the airport. I was there in no time.

I walked up to their front desk, court orders in hand. The building was old, having a musty and old oil-stained wood smell. I was nervous but filled with purpose. I *was* going to get that information. I asked for the social worker that I had spoken with on the phone, and the receptionist asked if I had an appointment.

I smiled, saying, "She's expecting me." Well, it wasn't a lie.

I waited only a couple of minutes, and a professional-looking woman in her early forties greeted me. She seemed to be much nicer in person than she was on the phone. I was invited into a back office. We talked for maybe an hour, mostly about me. Questions went back and forth with her wanting to know the reason for my search. There I sat discussing my life and how secure I was with myself because of my relationship with God. I told her I had accepted Jesus as my Lord and Savior in 1986 and knew who I was because of Him. We talked about my adopted parents and how much I loved them. I needed to know medical information about my biological family. However, I wanted to find my birthmother just to say thank you for my life.

It was funny how the conversation sounded as though I was listening outside myself, like listening to another person. Then the social worker said, "Since you are going to find your mother, I think you should know about the father." She paused and looked at me with no hint of emotion while I realized I hadn't given him much thought.

Then the words came like a brick hitting me right in the face. She didn't yell, but she might as well have.

"Your mother was raped!"

In an instant I was crying for my mother's pain. I walked out of the office but really don't remember how. I don't even remember those final words with the social worker. The next moment I was fighting for my life against demons of old. The voices that had told me I was worthless all my life seemed to gain power with my knowledge of how I was conceived. That's when I found myself surrounded by those voices as I sat in the car.

I sat there, exhausted from the fight to survive the pain of all that I had been told. Now that the voices had stopped, I numbly started the car. At first it was my mother's pain that had tears erupting. But now as I drove back to the airport, it was my own excruciating pain that kept the tears pouring out. Reality forced itself back on me. The fantasy of everything running smoothly came crashing down. I wasn't going to be able to hide my emotions this time.

I arrived at the airport with swollen eyes, and it took no genius to figure out something had gone terribly wrong. Shocked and confused my husband asked, "What happened?"

"I *don't* want to talk about it!" I snapped.

"I'm supposed to be your best friend, so *tell* me," he demanded.

Filled with furious anger and a tight fist demonstrating a punch, I spouted, *"If you don't leave me alone, I am going to punch you in the face!"*

The shock alone kept him silent for over an hour. In our past we had experienced problems with our relationship, and I'm sure Richard had thoughts of his own running through his head. Would this be used to take us back to the days when we fought all the time?

There is evil that is always trying to use things to get the biggest bang against us. If it can affect one person, then it has a chance of playing dominoes to affect multitudes of others. I was certainly passing on my pain at that moment. As my crying subsided, Richard once again attempted to communicate. Just because my crying was controlled didn't mean I was fine and dandy. In fact, I was a volcano waiting to erupt. The look I gave him said it all, and he made no other attempt to question me. We sat in silence waiting to board the plane. My anger and hurt was great as I sat there. I noticed a young man wearing a vulgar, woman-degrading T-shirt. I wanted to jump all over that man, but I just sat there seething. Had I not been a Christian with restraints, I would have attacked him physically at that point. We wonder how some people can go nuts and kill people in a mall or school. No one really knows the power evil possesses. Thoughts can get out of control. This is why the Bible says to take every thought captive. We are not safe unless we have the power greater than evil.

Lies running through my head played on and on. I was angry, helpless, and seemingly hopeless living on this earth. I didn't focus on the power I had to overcome, which is available to all believers in Christ. I just felt restrained, not powerful. All I looked forward to was death and being done with all this. I didn't want to talk to family or anyone else. Once open to the world, I was now closed to everyone and everything.

———

My life played back in my mind like a movie now, the good and the bad. The good was that at three months of age, I joined a WWII veteran and his wife to start their family. Before my mom passed away in 2001, my parents had been married almost sixty years. My dad's humor and patience had held it together during my mom's ongoing illness and constant pain. That was very good. Together they agreed to tell me at the age of six that I was adopted. Affirming me with love, they assured me I was chosen and so special. That was *very* good. I always liked remembering when my mom would say good night, she'd always add, "Go to sleep knowing I love you; wake up knowing I love you. Because I *do* love you." Another good memory was when my parents would tell the story of how well I knew how special I was even at the young age of three. I was in the back seat of the car when a horsefly flew in one day. Scared, I yelled for my dad to kill it. He assured me it was harmless, but I was not convinced and told him, "If you don't kill it and I die, you know you can't afford to get another little girl!" This example shows that even at an early age, we value life. There is an instinctual struggle to live. But sometimes things happen to make us lose that truth. This is the bad side of life.

I learned about life from the ground up growing up as a farmer's daughter! I watched as life was formed, served its purpose, and then was no more. I was taught right from wrong and respect for others. However, harsh times tried to leave me bitter. Because my mom was very strict and very ill, she did things that hurt me deeply and on one occasion left me suicidal. These were the bad times and the thoughts I kept going back to. At thirteen I looked into her medicine cabinet and considered taking all the medications to end my emotional pain. I heard distinctly in my head, "Forgive her because she doesn't know what she is doing." I closed the medicine cabinet and chose to forgive. After finding out how my life had begun though, thoughts were telling me I should have taken those drugs to end it all. I just didn't want to live anymore. For many years I had lived with forgiveness toward my adopted mom. But at this time I was reliving and grasping for pain to justify my worthlessness.

Yes, there were good times, but I had chosen to focus on the bad times that had left me confused, hurting, and doubting my worth. As a teen I struggled with self-esteem, as all teens do. Personal identity is a real struggle for any teen. My struggles bore the added weight of birth-mother's abandonment. Then there were times when my adopted mom would say or do something ugly that made me think she didn't love me as her own. I am sure now that her pain did a lot of the talking. I didn't know at the time that some people, like my mom, don't know how to gain control over the pain they feel. Everyone around is made to feel their pain, and then there is a domino effect of hurts. Now I was choosing to remember only the negatives and passing on my pain to those around me. My mind searched for more memories to continue the pain. I was in a passive self-destruction mode. I wouldn't put a knife to my wrist, but I would continue torturing myself with these thoughts.

I had always wanted to know the truth, but now I didn't know what to do with it. Being told all my life that my mother had died at forty-six giving birth and now finding out that she was twenty-two and had been raped was devastating. My adopted parents had been told that story for fear that they wouldn't want to adopt a rape baby. It is sad that children like me are considered "throwaways"! After being told the truth, I felt like I was being sucked into that stigma of worthlessness and having no reason for living.

My mom's actions didn't always line up with her words of love, so I struggled to know real love. Now I was struggling for my life's purpose. Sure, I knew it in my head, but I didn't feel it. I knew that God loved me but couldn't reason why.

My adopted mom was insecure and passed that inse-curity on to me. For many years, I think she felt threatened by my wanting to know my birthmother. Many times adopted parents feel that way and even fear losing the child to the birthmother. Sometimes the children suffer from the way they are "protected." But what adoptive parents need to know is that their children love their adopted parents like any other child loves a parent. We don't know any different. When we have conflicting messages between words and actions, any child will become confused, but adopted children even more so.

Then on our side we are so afraid to offend our parents with trying to find our birthmother. It feels almost disrespectful. So many children postpone finding the birth family until very late in life. Sometimes they don't even want their adopted parents to find out for fear that they will be upset. There are multitudes of emotions in an adopted child's mind. One thing is certain—our adopted parents *are* our parents!

I loved my adopted parents as any biological child would. I knew nothing else. I did wonder so often, though, why was I given away. My parents had no idea of the truth of my beginnings. Because of the stigma involved in "cases" like mine, it was probably better that they didn't know at the time of adoption. Certainly it was best that *I* didn't know in my younger years.

Years ago, unmarried pregnant girls carried a heavy burden because it was not accepted like it is today. So many adoptive parents were told "stories." My younger adopted brother came with the same type of legitimizing story. His story was that his birthmother was married but wanted a career and not a child. He is three years younger than I am and has gone back and forth with wanting to know his birthmother. I always wanted to know. I never vacillated. Never being impressed with fame or wealth, I didn't care what my birthmother did, so much as whom she was. I longed just to thank her.

—

Life was difficult with my adopted mom in constant pain. Verbal attacks from her, along with physical punishments, were frequent. While I understood her pain, I carried my own pain of feeling rejected.

It's said that laughter is the best medicine. So I learned early to hide pain and make people laugh. It made me feel good too. It sure beat having them laugh *at* me. I was the class clown. I'd get in trouble, teachers would tell my parents, and then I'd get in trouble at home too. I just wanted attention. A lot of times that's what kids do. They either act out with silliness or rebellion. I chose silliness knowing my mother would not tolerate the rebellion. Laughter was far from my thoughts now as I ran through the events of my life.

I tried to think of my father. My dad was a great man and showed his love and affection to me. He could tolerate far more than my mom could. He was a man of great honor. He fought in WWII and was even standing next to the men as they raised that famous flag at Iwo Jima. He was always happy, and I did feel loved by him. I have great memories with my dad. My adopted parents were faithful to go to church every Sunday, and we knelt to say our prayers every night together as a family. However, it is sad how bad feelings press out the good if you let them. And I did just that. I chose to dwell on this world instead of what eternal joy I had available to me. I even tried to think about God. I had seen God's hand protect me and provide for me over my life. He loved me enough to die for me. I had seen miracles. But here I was reaching for every idea that would prove that He didn't love me.

Looking back, while I was hurting so badly, I couldn't or *wouldn't* focus on the positive. But as I look back today, I see how slowly I learned. My adopted mom always said I'd have to learn the hard way. Some of us do have to experience life this way, but others will catch on quickly. Some won't take the advice or warning from others who know the pain. They see it as preaching and miss the opportunity to avoid Satan's traps in the journey of life.

My prayer is that you would use what I have learned to help you live your life burden free and focused on God Almighty. Certainly, I do not know it all. I am sharing what I have learned. I will use what others learned to make my own life better. It is only a fool who thinks he knows everything and will not listen to those who have traveled down the same road. Ignore warning signs on a road, and it could be fatal. This is true of our spiritual road too.

I could easily divulge my difficulties, as there would be many of you who could identify with all my trials. However, rather than dragging you through every detail of my past, I will only use events to show life wasn't easy for me and overcoming is a choice. Too many times people relive those treasures of the devil and take others with them. I neither want to go there myself nor do I want to paint detailed ugly pictures in your mind.

Well, back home from the trip to the adoption agency, I still felt emotionally dead. I managed to tell my husband, but I still refused to open up completely. Sleep came easily that night, but morning came much too soon. Nothing had changed. My stomach ached along with my heart.

I thought I would have to live like this forever. I couldn't see past the moment. Every movement was forced. I had to live because my life wasn't my own. I was lying to myself, however, in that this was life. Yes, I was breathing, but this was not living for Jesus the way He deserved. But that's all I had in me to do at the time. It was all I could do to get up in the morning and start moving. My children, my husband, my art—nothing had meaning anymore. Since I had determination to go on with my life, I moved on, no matter how robotic.

Having written a few songs, I had previously scheduled time with a composer to work on one of them. Singing and writing didn't really matter to me at this point, but I decided to keep my appointment. This was the next day after the trip, only hours after learning I was conceived in rape.

Feeling sure I could pull off a great act, I set out on my one-hour drive. I had plenty of time to think, but nothing seemed to process in my brain. Just empty darkness filled my mind. There were really no thoughts.

I finally arrived at the composer's home. I switched into my actor mode and walked in as though nothing had happened. I was confident that she'd be fooled into thinking all was well with me. She was unaware of my horror the day before. After some chitchat, she said she had just finished a song for someone else and wanted me to hear it. To my great shock, my world came crashing down to the tune of a song about using and losing women. I can't even tell you now what the words were exactly. But I was hit hard. Before I knew what I was doing, I screamed, "*Shut up. Stop it!*" putting my head between my knees. I was crying so hard, I thought the darkness around me was because I couldn't see through the tears.

Suddenly I saw a vision of myself falling into a deep dark abyss, deeper and deeper, blacker and blacker.

The composer jumped off her piano bench and without hesitation said to me, "I don't know what you're going through, but *God knew you before you were ever conceived.*"

Immediately I saw a hand reach down in this vision, grab my arm, and catapult me into a brilliant light. I knew she could have used any combination of a million words, but God had placed these in her mouth just for me. With the greatest joy and freedom I have ever felt, I raised my head, looked straight into her eyes, and said, "I believe it!" What a transformation! If this is only a fraction of the intensity of meeting Jesus face to face, everything in me longs for that great day. My whole being went from death to life in an instant! The composer told me she witnessed a true miracle. When I first started screaming, she thought I was having a nervous breakdown. Well, I was. She wondered if she should call an ambulance at first. Immediately after speaking to me, she knew God had taken over. My life was now real and filled with purpose. I was not formed by a man, but by the very breath of God—as is every human. The moment I *believed*, fifteen of the most horrible hours of my forty-five years suddenly turned to abundant joy. It was incredible and I never felt more alive. God himself touched me. In as little as fifteen hours from the time I got the information about my conception, I was totally free! All things are possible with God. One does not need to spend years seeking freedom. It is a choice to believe freedom is yours for the taking.

MEETING MY BIRTHMOTHER, SEEING GOD AT WORK

What is the value of life? Where does it come from? Does it have value if it isn't planned? Can man or woman really create life? If so, why doesn't everyone who wants to have a child get pregnant? Why do women who don't want a baby get pregnant?

People ask so many questions. Maybe you too have asked one or more of these questions.

Consider for a moment the complexity of life. In the instant an egg is fertilized, that embryo has *all* the DNA information to determine what that human will be and look like. Amazing. If you were to look at it under microscopic lenses, you would actually see what looks like machines at work, constructing everything in that blueprint given by the DNA.

Undoubtedly this is beyond happenstance or accident. It looks like any other manufacturing plant complete with delivery trucks, carriers, and buildings. Of course I am using my own language for this, but it's easy to identify these participants in the program. Everyone would agree that when we see a manufacturing plant, we know it is there by engineering and design, not from some big bang!

So I dare say it is a forced and determined conclusion

to say that we are accidents after looking at the incredible evidence of design. While we can destroy life with our eyes closed, something happens when our eyes behold the beauty of it all.

Sitting on my couch one Friday night in November 2005, I was enjoying a TV program called *Three Wishes* with Amy Grant. I loved seeing wonderful dreams come true for these people. This particular night was quite interesting to me and kept me on the edge of my seat.

There was a young woman wanting to find her birthmother. She had no information at all. All she knew was that she was adopted. Of course, by the end of the show, she had been reunited with her birthmother.

Well, I was crying tears of joy for her, mixed with sadness that I had not found my own birthmother. I had paid someone $2000 in Arizona years ago and got absolutely nothing for it. I didn't even get much correspondence. When I questioned the woman she told me everyone can't be found.

I was already disappointed, but I jumped off the couch when they named the company Amy Grant had used. I ran to my computer and searched for Worldwide Tracers Ltd., and there it was. I immediately emailed them and waited for them to contact me.

Early on Monday, I was hard at work antiquing a wrought iron door when a call from Worldwide Tracers Ltd. came. I was so excited because I had information they could use. So I paid them right then. I was told I would have to give them a call back because they didn't make calls to clients. Okay, no problem there.

Well, I was so scared that there would be no information. So I waited three weeks to call them back.

I practiced my script over and over of what I would say to my mother if they did find her. The man working on my case said they almost always contacted the mothers, but I told him I wanted that privilege. I didn't want her scared off before I had the chance to say thank you to her. I knew that I would get only one chance and didn't want to blow it. They said I seemed to be very sure of myself in not wanting to hurt my mother, so they agreed.

I was painting a model home for a designer when I decided to make the call to the agency. I made the call to Worldwide Tracers Ltd. during my lunch break. When I was told that the agency had an address, my screams of joy could be heard throughout the house. At first everyone looked at me like I was crazy. I was dancing around like I had ants in my pants. But once I told everyone the story, they too were excited for me.

I left the job right then, packed, and got on a plane to my birthmother's address. My plan was to knock on her door and say, "Hi, I'm looking for Ann. I have a message for her from my mother. She has passed away and wanted Ann to know this." I was expecting to get in easily this way.

I arrived at the house with a gorgeous bouquet of flowers in hand and my heart in my throat. I couldn't walk up to the door fast enough. It was a small wooden house in a quiet older neighborhood. Trees were vibrantly colored and it smelled like fall.

I knocked at the door and waited. There was a cute black and white cat peeking through the window of the door. That was the only greeting I received. So I just decided to drive around a bit, get something to eat, and come back.

I came back at about two o'clock, and still no one was there. I waited till five p.m., and a car drove into the driveway. Before the woman could get out of the car, I was there ready to speak to her. She looked at me strangely, and I said, "I'm looking for Ann."

To my great disappointment the young woman said, "There is no one by that name living here."

"But this is the address I have for her," I said, hoping there was some reason for the mistake.

"I've had the house for two years. I don't know who had it before because I bought it from a realtor," she replied.

"Sorry to have bothered you," I said, slowly walking away.

No, this could not be happening. I was so tired of this. Up then down, then up, then down again. I was exhausted. The smell of the flowers I bought for my mom only depressed me more. Now what? The only thing I knew to do was to call a friend in Houston who was a private investigator. I wanted to cry, but she encouraged me not to leave the city until I had searched the courthouse for records. "Go to the neighbors too. They have to know something if she lived there for thirty plus years." She managed to give me energy to go on. I had hope again, though my ups weren't going as high now.

The neighbors on each side of my birthmother's house had no clue because they were fairly new also. Strike two, and I was determined now to keep going. Third time was a charm, and a nice gentleman invited me into his home to talk. He knew of them because he too had lived there many years. He told me about my mom being sick a lot. I didn't let on that I was her child. I kept the story going about having a message to deliver. He told me she was now in a nursing home, but he had no idea which one. He suggested I go to another neighbor who "knew everything that went on." I did, and she was a bit suspicious. She didn't know anything but said she'd take my number and call me if she had anything.

I couldn't go to the courthouse until the morning, so I went back to the hotel after I got something to eat. My stomach was upset from being nervous. I just couldn't seem to sleep more than an hour without waking. I'd be so glad when morning finally came. Though I had my doubts, morning did come, and I was off to do research. This proved to be fun.

After telling everyone in the records area about my story, I found favor, and everyone wanted to help me. One looked downstairs, and another took me upstairs, where we found a probated will for my grandmother. Wow, it was like finding treasure. I found names and addresses of my birthmother's two brothers.

I tried calling one but got no answer while the other had an answering machine. I certainly wasn't going to leave a message. I don't know if their phone showed how many times I called, but it must have been thirty times before I got on the plane to fly back home.

I walked through the airport in a daze with my huge bouquet of flowers. One man even said to me, "Wow, you must be loved." I replied, "Yeah, by me." I then told him what had happened, and he too looked disappointed for me. But I added, "God loves me too."

We both smiled.

Back at home, Richard pushed me to call once more. This time I got someone on the phone. Faye was my mother's sister-in-law. *Show's on*, I told myself. "Hi, my name is Juda Myers, and I am looking for Ann. I know that you're her sister-in-law. Can you tell me how to contact her?"

Faye was very curious and began asking questions. "Why do you want her?"

"My mom passed away and wanted me to give Ann a message. She really blessed my mom." Without hesitation I answered just as I had practiced.

"What was your mother's name?" she asked.

Right back I said, "Alma."

Strongly she said, "I don't know that name. I went to school with Ann, and I know all those people."

No problem, I thought. "This wasn't in high school."

"Oh?" she said slowly and with questioning in her voice. She hesitated. I knew the wheels were turning in her head. "Where *did* your mother know Ann?" she said even slower.

"In Louisiana," I again answered with ease.

Then there was the loudest silence I have ever heard. Thoughts were now running through *my* head. She knew, and I knew that she knew.

Then she broke the silence with "I'll have to get my husband to call you."

I faked a nonchalant comment—"Oh, no problem. Here's my number."

I hung up the phone and was convinced I'd never hear from her again. It was over, and I would never find my mother. Not ye of little faith, but one of *no* faith! I just gave up.

Fifteen minutes later my aunt called back. She had called Ann and given her my number. Ann was having issues and wouldn't be able to call for a couple of months. I talked to Faye about knowing she was in a nursing home and asked if Ann was okay. Ann had COPD and some other problems. I thanked Faye for doing this for me, and we hung up.

Would I ever hear from her? God only knew. This was a Friday, and I chose to just forget about it. I had a new plan. If I ever got a call, I would not answer. I'd take the number and do a cross-reference on the Internet to locate the address. I wanted to just show up there and not give her the chance to reject my meeting her.

I was once again painting, as this was my profession. The Tuesday following my conversation with Faye, I was at my pastor's house about to begin painting murals. A call came through, and I was truly caught off guard. I knew it was my birthmother. Oh my goodness, now I really was excited. But I couldn't answer the phone. She would leave a message, I was sure. And she did. I hurried to hear it.

"Hi, this is Ann. Sorry I missed you. I will try to call Richard."

Oh no, I couldn't let her do that and have him pick it up. He would ruin everything. I immediately called Richard and told him not to answer. I began trying to tell my pastor's wife about the whole story, but my sentences ran together. I probably didn't make much sense to her. She is a sweet, quiet little woman. She must have thought I had lost my mind as I explained without breathing that I must go. Then off I went.

It was still early when I arrived back at home from the pastor's house. I didn't even get started on my painting. I was out of breath when I asked my dad if he'd like to hear my birthmother's message. My dad was living with us at the time. Dad was perfectly healthy, but we thought it would be nice for him to live with us after the death of my mom. I was really happy that he could share the joy of finding my birthmother.

As I played the message for my dad, I stared at him in amazement. We both listened as we heard *all* of her message. When I first listened at the pastor's house, I had hung up the phone immediately after she said she would call Richard. I did not hear the rest of her message.

"If you are who I think you are, I want to see you." My eyes widened. "If you are my long lost daughter, Mary Beth, God bless you; I want to see you. And if you're not, God bless you anyway. I want to know what you want."

Wow! She *wanted* to see me. Was I dreaming? I was all over the place, literally jumping for joy. My dad always had a smile on his face, but now it was bigger than I'd ever seen. I took the phone into my bedroom for privacy. Something always made me want to be alone for that moment I'd meet her. Even today I can't say what that was about. It was such an emotional time.

I called the number and waited as the phone rang. A nurse answered first, and I asked for Ann. If "butterflies in the stomach" describes nervousness, I am positive I had a herd of elephants in mine. This day was December 7, 2005, ten o'clock in the morning. Carolers were at the nursing home serenading the residents. My mother was given the phone. I started talking, but she said, "Honey, you're gonna have to speak up, I can't hear you."

So I said very loudly, "*As far as I know I'm your daughter!*"

At the very moment I was saying this, I heard the

caroling voices singing, "Glo-ooooo-ooooo-oooooria!" It was as though all of heaven was rejoicing with us.

Then my father got to speak to her. I just cried as I heard him thank my birthmother. "Thank you for giving me a beautiful daughter. I am so grateful. My wife couldn't have any children."

It truly was a blessing and dream come true. I just remember telling my birthmother I would be on the next plane. We didn't talk much on the phone that day because I wanted to talk in person. I couldn't stand it. I was all energy and wanted to tell everyone about the miracle I was walking in. This was not like the time I found out at the agency that I was conceived in rape. I felt beat down then, but now I had a testimony of God's working love. I had to share it. I told my story to anyone who glanced my way. Each time I got the same reaction. They would gasp. Some would have big smiles while others had tears. But all shared my joy and wanted to know the whole story. The flight seemed to go quickly as I talked to the passenger next to me. He listened intently, marveling at what had happened. He was Jewish, and we talked about how God Yahweh is so good. Most assuredly He is. Upon arrival, I rented a car as fast as I could, hurrying to the nursing home. I didn't stop for flowers this time. I wanted to just get there for fear I'd awaken from a dream. I had thought, imagined, and planned for so long. Now it was happening. I felt as though I were living inside a movie script. It was all surreal.

My adoption records said my birthmother had brown eyes. My eyes are bright blue and have been the focal point of what people remember about me. I was so worried that I might look like the rapist and bring back all that pain on this wonderful woman. After what she had done for me, I couldn't bear the thought of hurting her in any way.

I managed to get a flight only a few hours after talking with Ann. I arrived at the nursing home at seven p.m. I stood in front of the reception desk about to ask for Ann when I heard my name. "Juda?" I turned around to see eyes I had only seen in a mirror looking back at me. Yes, she had bright blues too. I hugged her and we cried for joy. It was wonderful. She was in a wheelchair but filled with life and joy. The whole nursing staff knew about me and celebrated our reunion. My birthmother had told them nine months prior upon her arrival to the home that she had given a baby girl up for adoption. She had never forgotten nor had she stopped talking about me.

Was this all really happening? God was so good to me. Not all reunions are a dream, as some are more like a nightmare. Not all are able to see the truth that a baby is a baby. The baby has no guilt in any part of this crime or *any* other situation where a woman or girl gets pregnant. We are not created out of our own will. We have no choice of our own to be born, and my birthmother knew this completely.

After about an hour talking to my birthmother, I had the courage to ask, "Do you mind telling me how I was conceived?" I didn't want to cause her any pain, but I wanted to know the truth. Since the adoption agency lied about other things, I had to know the truth directly from the source.

Without hesitation she told me exactly what happened. "I was raped by eight men while walking home from seeing the Ten Commandments." I burst into tears and buried my face in her lap as I knelt down in front of her. She patted me on the shoulder and in an upbeat tone said, "Honey, stop your cryin'. That was a long time ago, and I've forgiven those men. And look what God has done. He's brought you back to me. God is faithful!"

Wow, what a woman! What an example of joy through forgiveness. I dried my eyes and saw a different world appear. I was so proud of her. She said she was proud of me too and that I shouldn't feel badly about what happened. It was not my fault. "You were just a baby," she assured me. I too would forgive, as she and God wanted it.

We visited with staff and told a group of student nurses about our reunion. They listened with eyes widened with amazement. Ann even instructed them to give any baby life if they found themselves in an unwanted pregnancy. She said, "It's a baby!" About two hours before I had to leave, I decided to contact the local TV station. I told them I realized there wasn't much time, but if they were interested in a good story, they should come by the nursing home. They were ecstatic and rushed over in twenty minutes. When they arrived, the reporter and the cameraman both said with excitement that they "lived for these kind of stories." And so came the first interview. My birthmother was a natural, although she said she was shy and hesitated at first. But the minute I said she might be able to save another baby with her story, she said, "Let's do it!" She was bold with her words, telling the audience not to have abortions because it was murder of an innocent child.

The station edited that part because they said it would be too harsh. While that is the truth, I realize some of you reading this have had an abortion and feel the pain of that truth. There is also more wonderful freeing truth for you. The truth is that God loves you personally and can forgive you if you ask. Freedom is only a whisper away. *Ask Him to forgive you and then forgive yourself.* That is freedom, and it is available to any and all who ask. Nothing is too great for God to forgive!

Don't be burdened down with this weight. It drags you down and keeps you from your destiny. Truth is, God has so much more for you. But you are the one blocking the blessings, not Him. Know the truth, and the truth will set you free.

When I was having that nervous breakdown and the composer told me God knew me before I was conceived, I already knew that. However, I did not experience freedom until I grasped that truth for myself and *believed* it. Without it you will only stay in darkness and hopelessness. The next chapters will help anyone wishing to break free from their own darkness. They help to identify feelings, provide actions that lead to freedom, and offer inspiration through the lives of others who found freedom in forgiving.

RETELLING, RELIVING, AND RELEASING THE PAST

Sometimes it is good to remember the past, loved ones, and happy times. We all want to remember those times. Those are great for retelling and for reliving. These bring warm feelings and experiences that help others grow. Times with the family laughing and sharing will bond generations together as the stories of old are replayed. Remembering good times gives us hope that the future will bring more good times. The Bible tells to us to write God's laws on our foreheads and remember them. "Fix these words of mine in your hearts and minds; tie them as symbols on your hands and bind them on your foreheads" (Deuteronomy 11:18–25). That is to press them into our thoughts. Also we should remember all the good God has done lest we forget and become bitter, turning away from Him. Everyone loves a great story. You are reading this book probably because you thought it would be a great story to inspire you. That is the kind of retelling that brings life to others. We can experience it all over again to relive the moment in the retelling.

But what about the bad times? What should we do with those? Choosing our thoughts is a learned process and might take some practice. Here is an analogy of the mind needing the body to practice to make thoughts happen. People laugh at me when I tell them the story of my elliptical stairclimber. My husband gave it to me as a Christmas present. "Oh no, you didn't," I protested. I didn't want that thing. He said I needed it as I "got older" to keep my heart in shape. And again I said, "Oh no, you didn't tell me I am getting older!" I wasn't out of shape to look at but knew I was a wimp when it came to exercise. I *hated* it. I used to be so active when I was younger, but now I was tired with little desire or time to waste on this machine. So one day I thought I would give it a try. I was horrified. Twenty *seconds!* Yes, that's right, only twenty seconds on that monster, and I was dying. You know the look—red and blue splotches in the face, perspiration glistening (women don't sweat, you know), hunched over in a pile ready to faint. This was going to be impossible even though I went in thinking I would simply not like the experience. You know the feeling you get cleaning the toilets. It just has to be done. But I couldn't even "get 'r done"! My mind said I could, but my body would need practice and conditioning. It is hard work. Some of us have just as hard of a time conditioning ourselves to not retell everything. It will take practice, but it can be done. As I remember the past to show you it is possible to overcome, I am forced to choose to relive it or simply retell it. I have made a conscious decision to release the punishment mentality against my offender before I retell the stories.

Is it possible to retell without reliving? With God all things are possible. He can even erase memories for you if you are unable. But He wants us to make the effort. Some things we must do for ourselves, just like a butterfly will die if you help peel away the cocoon. We will be stronger to work through our own thoughts, giving us self-control, accessible at any time we need it.

How do you know whether you are retelling or reliving? You will know by your reactions afterward. Can you maintain peace as though you are telling someone else's story, or are you bombarded with all the emotions as though it just happened? You will know that you have released it all when it no longer has control of you.

Why do we have to tell anyway? Is it just to have something to talk about? People are all different. Some even choose not to talk about it because it hurts too much. Others talk to get back at the offender, and still others just want pity. For some people, talking will be wrong, and for others talking will be right. Here are some questions to help illustrate right and wrong.

I ask myself these questions before retelling a story about an offense.

> Will this make me angry?
> Am I still hurting when I talk about it?
> Is this meant to expose the offender?
> Will I be a prisoner of my thoughts again?
> Will the listener be hurt also?
> Am I trying to form a group for myself that is against the offender?

If you answer yes to one or more of these when you tell your story, then you need to stop talking about it. Don't talk about your offender while you are still in this frame of mind. You will do no one any good, especially yourself. You must be able to release the offender before you can consider talking about it. If you need to tell someone for counseling sake, be very selective of the person you tell.

I suppose *my* test will be in writing this. I believe I will retell experiences, but I'll know only after I write this if I am as free as I think. I know I want to hurt no one. That is gone, and I have released my offenders. But sometimes there lingers one or two strings that tug at us. When I want to talk about an offender, I too must ask those same questions. If there is a lingering, I must state that I release that offender and ask God to forgive me and them. I must ask God to forgive me for hanging on. I must forgive my offender so that I can receive my freedom.

I recall someone in ministry taking advantage of my talents, never even noticing that they did anything wrong. My husband saw it and was also disappointed with that person. I had the choice to keep it to myself or tell everyone. Telling everyone would expose this person and make others think badly also. I chose to protect that person. I did tell a couple of close friends that didn't know this person and one person that did. The one that knew the person was mature enough to *not* treat the offender differently or tell others.

Be careful to share your offense only after prayer and consideration. A part of me wanted justice, but the side of me that is the image of God wanted to protect my offender. If I caused another person to harbor feelings toward my offender, then this evil would have spread throughout the church. This wasn't an offense that needed a police intervention, so there was no reason to expose that person. It would have only made evil grow, which I claim to despise. "See to it that no one misses the grace of God and that no root of bitterness grows up to cause trouble and *defile many*" (emphasis added) (Hebrews 12:15). I must not let my bitterness defile others. Just the fact that the Bible tells us not to let it happen means that it *does* happen.

My actions must line up with my desire to do what is right. Even in this writing I am careful not to expose this person. I treated my offender with love and respect even though they hurt me. I have the peace knowing I did what pleased God and what keeps me growing in the right direction. God has been good to me, not exposing all my sins to the world. I *must* appreciate that gift enough to share it with others! Think about that for a while. How many of us have done things and don't want the spotlight shining on us? Ever heard the saying (which used to be the golden rule) "Do unto others as you would have them to do unto you"?

Some of you will also think back on similar memories as mine. If they create such bitter emotion for you, then ask the Lord to free you as you let go and forgive those who have hurt you. No one can go through life without being hurt by another human. Whether the person is aware of the pain they caused makes no difference. Most offenders will even justify themselves if you confront them. So then what? You still have a choice.

If you have been offended, you are a receiver. Receivers have the option to receive or not to receive. The person receiving is *always* in control. A receiver decides whether to keep the injury or heal and move on. If your television receiver doesn't work, you will see nothing playing. If *you* don't "receive," you won't *have* the offense. That goes two ways. If you do not receive the "bad," you won't be stuck with it. But if you don't receive "good," then you won't live free either. Again that word—choice. Life isn't a passive thing. Things are happening either to you, for you, or with you. *You* make that choice. If you choose to not "receive" the offenses, then you won't have anything to "relive or retell." Releasing the past through forgiveness is how this is achieved.

⁓

We relive the past with voices in our heads trying to talk us into doing many things. How we think about things can help us to release the past or push us to continue being affected by that past. When we are hurting we are more prone to listen to the bad voices. Drugs were never an issue for me except the time I considered using them to end my life at thirteen. In my mind I had thought I couldn't bear the humiliation and rejection from my mom. So I considered doing something I wouldn't normally think of doing. All I could think of was, *I can't take it anymore!* How many of us have said that or had that whispered in our ears? Satan hopes he will convince us we're finished and that we can't go on. If he can destroy us we will never know the love of God or His victory. But as I stood in front of the medicine cabinet thinking it over, I heard in my head, "Forgive her because she doesn't know what she's doing." How we act on our thinking is always *our* choice. The good thoughts that guide us are from God. He was guiding me to Himself. He gave me strength to live. God made it easy for me to forgive. It was always on my part to choose and act on it, though.

Many things in my life caused pain for me. Here are a few that came in my childhood. I can only talk about them now that I am free from the bitterness and unforgiveness. I am sharing these experiences for the sake of showing the difficulties I had to overcome.

This is a story that I can retell without reliving. There is just a memory without a pounding heartbeat or hurt-filled emotions. An obedient child most of the time, I was often accused of things I didn't do. This left me feeling defensive and angry. One time I was accused of trying to kill my mom. I was deeply hurt, especially having to take punishment for this accusation. She was allergic to perfumes. I had many tiny bottles of perfume simply as a collection of unusual bottles. They were never opened. I'm not sure why, but she accused me of wearing some. She actually believed I was trying to kill her by wearing perfume. She could see the bottles weren't opened, but there was no convincing her otherwise. Bitterness began taking root in my life for the things that were done to me. It was so subtle that I didn't even realize that it was happening. I did not try to kill my mom and was not hesitant in speaking my thoughts. That to me was injustice, and injustice truly got to me. I hated being accused of doing wrong when I hadn't and worse was to be punished for it. So my mouth became my defense. Actions reveal unforgiveness and hurt to others, but it is hard to see it in ourselves.

Speaking my thoughts got me in trouble. I had a strong will and started making deliberate choices, but not necessarily for the better. I started thinking that I wouldn't allow anyone to hurt me again. Ever thought those thoughts? Closing yourself off from others is a sign of harboring unforgiveness. Sure, we are able to function, but we aren't experiencing life to its fullest. It is like having an irritating splinter in our finger. When we touch it a certain way, it really hurts. That's like having unforgiveness dormant.

Something happens and we relive the past. A person who has not offended us can trigger this thought, and we lash out. Many times innocent people are paying the price for the original offender. I was determined to take control of my own life! However, I didn't realize that I was keeping some things while letting go of others. Other people were affected by my "triggers." I thought I was forgiving and even acting like it. I wasn't aware of the traces of lingering pain until I really came to know the Savior, Jesus Christ. That's when I became fully able to release all the past.

—

A truly serious offense happened to me when I was quite young. Satan tries to destroy people early, and if he can't get us one way, he does not give up. He is determined to find a way. He made me his target when I was only six years old. A fifteen-year-old neighbor molested me. It went on for about a year before my parents found out. Another neighbor saw something one day and told my mom. My innocence was stolen before I ever knew the meaning. Thus the seed was planted by the devil to create insecurity and inferiority. There are a great number of people suffering from a tree that has grown throughout their lives. It started from seeds planted years ago. Forgiveness is the only way to remove that tree of bitterness and hurt. Throughout my life people and events have brought me pain. *Anyone* who is living has experienced some type of pain, thus creating a need to be free.

This seed of bitterness in my life required nourishment. We retell, relive, but do not release past offenses. If we do not remove this seed early, it will demand to be fed so that it can grow. Things like anger, lust, and power are just a few of the things required to grow this tree. The tree's needs take over, and we substitute these things for what we really need, such as love, forgiveness, and purpose. Our true needs can only be totally fulfilled in the purpose and life of Jesus Christ. I cannot say that enough. Ever heard of "searching for love in all the wrong places"? Instead of releasing the past, we tend to substitute things like seeking wrong kinds of love. People may think they are in control, but truly that tree growing is in control. Every action is directed toward feeding the unforgiveness. Defensiveness, doubt, and insecurity are in control. I wanted to control, but I wasn't controlling myself, which is truly the only thing that can be controlled. I pretended to have it all together while dying inside.

There is a need in all our lives that only Jesus can fill. We sometimes go everywhere else to fill that need instead of running to the one who made the hole in the first place. We can say we aren't filling holes, but we put things in our mouth to fill a hole in our hearts. Or we shove needles in our veins to anesthetize our pain. Those things do not satisfy and can actually destroy the user. The root of the problem is always unforgiveness. How can I say that so assuredly? Ask a person that is in jail or takes drugs or is violent. They have a story that goes back to some point in their life where they were hurt and have not forgiven.

Small things can add up to hurts. Oddities in my own life, like not being able to wash my hair but once a week or not being allowed to wear makeup or pants, made me different at school. It was probably the smallest public school I have known, but people are people. My own class had twenty-eight students. No, that isn't a typo. The whole school from first through twelfth grade had 650 students. Everyone knew everyone and their families. I was embarrassed on many occasions by my mom and by students teasing me. The only things that kept me in the loop were my grades, my art, and my humor. People were afraid of my mom for obvious reasons. My mother's rules were set in stone but weren't necessarily for religious reasons. Others in my church wore makeup and pants. I was the only one who didn't. I felt alienated and thus confused and bitter as a teen. The way I dressed was the most noticeable difference from all other teens that went to school with me. While mini skirts and stockings were in, I wore dresses at my calves with socks. I didn't fit in like the rest, but somehow I survived and was liked. I tried to keep a happy attitude, but it was hard to maintain at times. My feelings fought between loving my mom and being bitter against her for her harsh treatment.

I remember a time when I was accused of cursing my mother. I did not even think of doing that, but she was convinced I did. So one Sunday after church, she determined I would be punished for this. She waited days to implement this punishment. She struck me in the face then proceeded to tell me I was going to lose my "precious hair."

"What for?" I questioned.

"You know!" she said.

But when I insisted I did not know, she told me it was for cursing her in the week. I protested, but she came back with, "Are you going to call me a liar too?" I couldn't win.

My hair was at the middle of my back and beautiful. She knew it was part of my identity and that all the other girls had long hair too. She forced me to sit down. Obediently, I sat there while she cut it all off. As I stood up I turned to her, and right there a root of bitterness was planted as I quietly said, "I hate you."

I went to my bedroom and looked at the freak in the mirror, tears rolling down my face. I was trying to comb the hair that was left when my mom came in threatening, "Leave it alone or I'll shave it off!" I knew she *wasn't* joking. This was one of the most humiliating times of my life. It took many years and a relationship with Jesus to uproot this tree that had grown for years. Sure, I acted as though all was fine, but the bitterness was a hidden poison in my life. Kids had laughed at me, and even teachers did too. Life just didn't seem to be worth living at the time.

We aren't taught about forgiveness. Sure, we are forced to say "Sorry!" But what does that mean? Kids walk off and harbor bad feelings. I am sure each one of us has a childhood story that is easily remembered. Children today can be taught how to forgive rather than just saying sorry. If we teach our children to forgive, just imagine what a better world we'd have. Their offenses would be released early in life and not drag on into their future and even to their children's future. Actions of unforgiveness and bitterness are learned too. What is better—to show anger and bitterness whenever something is triggered or to show peace and kindness to others through forgiveness?

My mother always said, "Someday you'll understand." It has taken a very long time. I don't agree with everything, but I do understand. I wish she would have taught me forgiveness. But she was in too much pain to do so. It is nearly impossible to help our children if we are not healed and have not forgiven.

As we are growing up, we may not understand the things that happen. Sometimes they are so hard, and they do plant that seed of bitterness. We have the choice to not let that seed grow.

Looking back I can see how all the hurts affect our lives. They engulf us, and we cannot step aside to see truth. We may not be able to prevent hurts in our life, but God has given us tools to work through them. His love and power enable us to overcome. *Figuring out everything is not possible, but overcoming is always possible.*

A relationship with Jesus Christ will give anyone the power they need to overcome. He is far beyond our understanding. We simply frustrate ourselves trying to figure Him out instead of trusting Him. Not trusting Him saps our power in Him. I clung to what I knew about God, making Him my reason to stay alive. I am now more than an overcomer, and you can be too.

While I had a lot of bad times, I did have my share of wonderful times. But our minds will dwell on how bad things are instead of the good if we allow it. The Bible says that God searches the earth for good. I want Him to stop and watch me doing good, like a little child wants her father to stop and watch her do something. Then I want to retell and relive all of that good. Then only the good will be left to affect other people.

Ever see a child do something and then say "look at me, Mommy" or "watch me, Daddy"? God longs to see His creation mimic Him just the way we love seeing our children look like us. He forgave us and longs to see us forgive others. Releasing the past is a God thing because He releases our past when we come to Him. Reliving past offenses breaks God's heart the same way our hearts break to see our children hurting.

God is a God of justice. So the longing for justice too is within us for a purpose. It is to long for the only one who is just and true. Where did the thinking of "it's not fair" come from? Evolution? No, I think not. The world says it is only survival of the fittest. But our hearts tell us something isn't fair! I bring up evolution to point out that we are not randomly created. There are aspects of our emotional being that evolution cannot explain. Evolution tries to dismiss a God who knows what is best for us. Humans tend to not want to be accountable to anyone else. When we acknowledge God, we have an endless supply of power to overcome any offense in life. Without Him we aimlessly wander through life trying to figure it.

I think that it is far better to do as God does. He searches for the good. We can't change our past, but we can control our right now and our future. Controlling thoughts enables us to control emotions, actions, and our life. Giving that power to someone or something else may end up in our destruction.

Imagine a time when your thoughts were uncontrolled, and you let someone upset you to the point of regret. You did or said something you wished you hadn't. That is letting someone else control you. You may be saying you can't stop someone from making you angry. Well, I say it doesn't have to last but a short time. You still have the choice of actions. The Bible says, "In your anger do not sin" (Ephesians 4:26). You have the choice to take every thought captive and *rethink* and direct your thoughts in a different direction. Have you ever seen someone get provoked with words until they were out of control? The more that person thought about the situation, the angrier they became. Maybe you have experienced that feeling. The thoughts continue as you relive it. Then it pushes you to retell it, forcing you to relive it again even as you retell it. It becomes a vicious circle that is fed by unforgiveness, anger, and bitterness. It must be released.

You can either sit behind the wheel letting someone else grab it and drive you somewhere they want to go, or you can take hold of it yourself and drive to the destination of *your* choice. If you are bitter about something and your bitterness grows when you talk about it, then *don't* talk about it. Wait until you are in control of those thoughts and know they won't take over. If anger happens with thinking about an offense, *do not open your mouth!*

I am not saying stick your head in the sand or never ever talk about it. Maybe you need to find someone who won't get you fired up but will listen and walk you through truth. Ask God to help you think His thoughts. Now, if you are not a believer in Jesus, the power to overcome evil completely is not available to you. You may have some times of relief, but it never truly goes away on your own power. Oh yes, you may see a few victories here and there, but something will pop up later. That may sound harsh, but I didn't make this up. I too had to choose to accept Jesus as my Savior first then immediately afterward accept Him as my Lord. Without that commitment to Him, there is no access to His power that defeats any and every evil. That's just the way things work.

Have you seen people without the power to quit a terrible habit that even they know is killing them? They do not *have* the *power.* They only have a power cord but have unplugged from the power source. Power from God enables a person to have peace beyond understanding and to walk in assurance and trust that God is in control no matter what life looks like. Sounds like a "crutch"? Why do people say things like that? Who on this earth can survive without something to hold them up? This kind of thinking keeps people from experiencing total freedom. Thinking we can do everything on our own is truly unrealistic.

Coming into this world as a completely dependent creature should make us realize we are not able to survive on our own. We *all* use some sort of crutch—work, money, self-talk, humor, sports, friends, and the list goes on. Some people don't acknowledge it, though. These crutches are not bad, but they represent the power cord without the power source or simply a battery-operated life. What happens when the limited power in those "crutches" die? Now if you have Jesus, that doesn't mean evil will disappear from the earth or from your life just yet. It does mean that you will no longer be linked to evil. Evil will no longer have your *mind.* The battle isn't in our bodies; it is in our minds. And that is where the change will have to begin. Seeking the one who made our minds is the best way to "fix" the problem of retelling and reliving the wrong events. The power to forever release the past is found only in Jesus.

Through His power I can forever retell the greatness, relive the moments of victory, and release those who have hurt me and the ones I love.

It's All in Our Head

You've heard it said, "As a man thinks, so he is." I guess this would attribute to one person physically capable but who out of fear never leaves the house. Another person, with no limbs, experiences joy touching lives all around the world. We look in total amazement at Nick Vujicic, who was born without arms and legs. He has led a more joyous, meaningful life than some people whom we might think to have everything going for them. Nick has taken his difficulties and given millions of people inspiration to make the most of their lives. People see him, and thoughts of self-pity and bitterness must be re-evaluated. He gives proof to the fact that one decides in his mind whether to be bitter or better. Pain happens; misery is a choice.

An example of the choices our minds have is evident with my adopted mom and her family. She was one of sixteen children—three boys and the rest girls. The fact that each one walked away as an adult with a different method of living attests to human individuality and mindset. It also proves we have a choice of coping with hardships and adversity. Within this family of sixteen, there were easygoing happy ones, hardened bitter ones, and those who were midway between the two, having coped with hardships in a positive way. What makes the difference? It's all in our heads.

My adopted mother was born somewhere in the middle of all these kids. Her life played back in her mind constantly. She repeated it to us weekly and even daily. She chose to replay the pain in her mind as well as pass it on to all those who would listen. Her own parents ruled with an iron hand; harsh, physical treatment was the norm. My mother talked constantly of how brutal my grandfather was to her and the rest of his children. He knew their names but didn't know which name went to each child. One story was told over and over again about the time my mom was pulled from the restroom and beaten. She bravely asked what her beating was for, and her father said that her mother told him to beat "M," her sister. When she said she wasn't "M," he brushed it off as nothing, saying she probably deserved a beating anyway. I knew these stories by heart.

Notice that term, "by heart"? What we hear and believe in our heads will be planted in our hearts. What we see goes to the mind and then transfers to the heart also. My adopted mother reinforced the heartache by replaying the tapes in her own mind. If it had only lived in her heart, that would have been bad enough. But it lived in her actions too. While she hated what was done to her, she couldn't see that her physical harsh treatment of her own children was wrong. No one could tell her she was wrong either. It was lodged deep within her mind, and there was no removing it.

She *chose* to protect those thoughts and would fight in anger if someone tried to remove them from her. All of the family knew she was holding on to things that were destructive. But she was the only one who could *choose* to change her thinking.

So I too lived with harsh treatment, hating my grand-father at one time for making my mom this way. As I grew older I realized it was *my* choice to be different, just as it was her choice to be the way she was. I would not carry this on to the next generation. There is an evil thread that Satan would love to weave throughout the generations. But God has set before each and every one of us life and death. He has given us a choice. But not only that, He has even told us the right one to choose. Why would He have to tell us? Shouldn't it be obvious? Well, it must not be, or God wouldn't have had to tell us.

Why do people take a wrong done to them and then do it to someone else? They have chosen death. In their minds they have taken what was put on them and chosen to make it their own through unforgiveness. It all starts in the head—in our minds.

Holding on to the wrongs others do to you kills you, the person created in the image of God (life in you). It then replaces that life and image of God with the image of death (revenge, hate, and bitterness). While clinging to the pain in your heart and allowing it to paralyze all that is good, you have now given your mind over to things that destroy you and those around you. This method of thinking is progressive and will only get worse. Know any miserable, bitter old people? They have piled years of misery high. They sit in the middle of all this ugli-ness unable to see above it. They never put the "garbage" out. Can you imagine never throwing *your* garbage away? You wouldn't think of it. But that may very well be what you've done with your garbage thoughts.

So you may be thinking you're not *that* bad, and you just don't want to be around the person who hurt you. Do you trust everyone the way you used to? If not, then you have taken away the chance to experience the possible good that God has to offer you through someone else. What if you are closing doors because in your own mind you see something bad happening all the time? How is it that some people can't forgive the smallest of things, but another man loves and cares for his father's murderer? Yes, that does happen, and it did for missionary pilot Nate Saint's son. He had a choice. He chose to believe God is truth and chose to forgive the man who drove a spear into his father, killing him. His choice began with his thinking. It was not instant, but he did choose to move forward in his forgiveness toward his father's killer.

Nate Saint wanted only to share goodness with natives but was killed because he was misunderstood. The attackers had never seen Nate and the three other missionaries before. They had no idea Nate was there to help them. He did not stop showing good even in the face of death. His mind had been prepared in advance to love and forgive. Nate's last word to his killer was "friend," spoken in their language.

Steve Saint, Nate's son, also made the right choice, though without a doubt one of his hardest decisions. Steve *chose* forgiveness for his father's killer. This decision has made him a free man filled with joy and contentment. It has also done something that he probably will never comprehend fully. In forgiving, he has set not only himself free but also the offender who wanted and needed that forgiveness. Then, through this story, so many others have been inspired to see their own potential for freedom, which continues the domino effect through all who are moved to change. Many lives have been changed by the movie *End of the Spear*[1] about Nate Saint's story, through the eyes of his son. Nate's killer and Nate's son, Steve, travel together sharing their story of amazing forgiveness. Hard to understand, isn't it? I will admit it is a mystery how this works, but it starts with our thoughts and the choice to do what is right through the power of God.

There is a God who has made the universe by no accident. He has a plan and knows what works and doesn't. Once we decide to follow the maker and His plan, we activate the real plan and purpose for our lives. Getting past all the noise in our heads is the hardest. But it still is our choice. What we think and dwell on is our choice.

Here's another example of God's truth in action, regardless of whether you're a believer or not. Oprah is an example of making a choice to change the wrong done to her by doing good for others. She doesn't talk often about the offenses done to her but instead focuses on how she can change her world for the better. She is taking others with her and is indeed changing people. Even if you do not believe in God's word, His law is still in effect, and people can reap the benefits on earth when they plug in. It feels good. There is a reward and a law put in place by God. Scientists have found that doing good sets off a warm fuzzy feeling inside our brains. But we must think it first before we can do it.

Some people miss this along the way, as forty-eight-year-old Simon Cowell of *American Idol* found out. He gave credit to Oprah on one of her television shows for having helped him to discover this "good feeling" phenomenon. Yes, giving makes you feel good. So if you aren't giving, for whatever reason you have in your mind, you will not receive the reward. I personally think God has put these laws and goodies in place to lead us to Him. He is the giver of all good and perfect gifts. However, some will just choose to use God's gifts and not give Him credit or follow *all* that He asks. There will be a day that He will make Himself known to everyone. I want to be found loving Him and loving His creation.

I know that if we are not accepted when we give our all to people, that in itself causes offense. We think it over and over—we feel cheated. We want to be appreciated. God has given His all when He sent His only son to be punished for the offenses we have done. Think about how He must feel to have given all He could and still not be recognized or loved. It will keep us from thinking we are the only ones that have been offended. Knowing and thinking about someone greater than ourselves, someone who suffered for us, makes it easier to forgive.

My birthmother made a choice to choose life for herself as well as for me. Her own mother wanted her to choose death. Abortion was set before my mom, and she chose life instead. For that I am grateful beyond words. She handed the choice to me, and I too am choosing life for myself. I choose to share that joy for life with those around me.

When eight men attacked and raped my birthmother, she had a choice to forgive or to take that link of death with her throughout her life. She did keep death—no forgiveness—for five years. It was one night when she was praying that she heard God tell her, "Ann, it's time to let it go." She said okay. She chose life again. Ann said yes to God. She took her thoughts captive and refused to continue thinking the way she did in the past. Her new way of thinking brought about her freedom. These are the thoughts I want to have in my head, thoughts of life and forgiveness that keep me living free.

If something terrible has happened to you, it is time to let it go. You aren't saying what was done is okay, but you are releasing the hold on your life that continues to cause damage. If you relive the moment, thinking it over and over, you are giving the offender even more time than they initially had. This is death. *Choose* to be free.

Some women who have experienced rape or other abuse have chosen to link up with this kind of death, allowing evil to take the life right out of them. Some women who have been raped are unable to even come out of their rooms. It's all in their head. I know that sounds harsh, but it truly is *their thinking that keeps them captive.* That is how one person can act like nothing happened and another closes off the world. We can choose to come out and defeat the enemy by living, even inspiring others to live too. Instead some people have chosen to stay in the moment of that crime against them. Like my adopted mother did, they relive their event over and over and over, never *growing*.

The enemy twists and perverts thoughts to keep us captive. He wants us never to know God's love or have the potential to love the way God intended. Some people cannot release their pain and their offender.

Here is a good illustration. Imagine yourself squeezing a snake that has just bitten you. You squeeze with all your might, and the snake bites you again. A trained snake handler tells you to let go, but you refuse. Since you are not strong enough to kill the snake yourself, you simply continue squeezing. The snake continues biting. Eventually you die, still holding the snake. The snake lives on! If you were to release the snake, you would also be released. But your thoughts keep you thinking you will overcome by seeking revenge. This is not ever successful.

The same happens with holding on to unforgiveness and reliving offenses. Let it go and give it to God who knows how to handle it. When we direct our thoughts to knowing truth, God steps forward to show us. Now thinking differently isn't about sitting cross-legged humming while going to your happy place. When you open your eyes, life will be waiting! So how do you change what's in your head?

While it's been said that seeing is believing, I have found that isn't always true. Carl Sagan admitted seeing no evidence of evolution, but he *chose* to believe it anyway. We choose to change our thoughts or not.

CHANGING YOUR THOUGHTS

To some it comes easy, but to others it is a daily, moment by moment decision. I once was very discouraged, not understanding the purpose for my circumstances. I desperately wanted to change everything around me. I could control nothing, not even myself. Wild outbursts after trying and trying only left me more frustrated for lack of self-control.

Years went by, and my family suffered too because of many reasons. I could blame my husband, but I suppose we were both to blame. Had I found my security in Jesus sooner, I would have spared myself the pain.

Raising children was a major point of disagreement, and because I hadn't dealt with my issues, I couldn't approach the topic with my husband properly. He had issues too, and together our arguments about discipline made it very hard on our two sons. Our thinking wasn't right.

Oh, to understand then what I know now. Self-control is definitely attainable, and I am living proof. But self-control did not come about until I gave control over to God.

We are impatient, especially in these days. We think we have to have what we want immediately, becoming frustrated and angry when it doesn't happen. In times past we watched slowly as our food was planted, cultivated, harvested, and then prepared to be eaten. All this took time and we learned patience. Today one has only to drive up to a sign with a microphone, speak what we want to eat, and then drive fifteen feet to pick it up. Have we gained anything? Maybe if we don't have time and must eat, this is gain. But in the long run it is not beneficial for us to continue this type of eating habit. So it is with thoughts. We are fed thoughts quickly, and we consume them, not evaluating what we have just taken in. If this is a constant way of life, we will suffer. *Just like some have begun to evaluate what they are putting in their mouths, we should also consider what we are putting into our minds.*

My husband and I were separated for one and a half years. I was happy or so I thought, not knowing I was settling for less than God's best. Praising God one day during my prayer time, I thanked Him for the divorce I wanted. I was absolutely shocked when God interrupted my thoughts with a most undeniable voice, "*I don't want that!*" I was shaking with fear.

The Bible tells us that the fear of the Lord is the beginning of wisdom. I must have been the smartest person on earth at that moment! I carefully asked, "What do you want?"

God wasted no time in telling me, "I want you to love him."

I burst into tears and said, "I hate him!"

Then I heard God say, "Treat him as though you felt the love."

I knew the voice of God, and I also knew that evil didn't ever want me to do anything good. So with a vision of a hard road ahead of me, I answered God, saying, "Because I love *you* more than anything, I will do it."

Oh, how I struggled, but I *chose* to control my thoughts. I chose to follow God and work toward *His* goal. It was only moments later that I took action to my commitment. I was determined not to let God down. *I was changing the way I thought.*

The call I made to my husband wasn't quite in the right attitude, but I was taking a step in the right direction. I began telling him I had heard from God. My husband wasn't happy when I told him God didn't want me to file for divorce. I then told him I was planning to be a winner in this no matter what he did.

> If he decided to divorce me, I would have peace in my house.
> If he moved back in and nothing changed, half my bills would be paid.
> If we both agreed to live for God, I'd be the happiest woman ever.

Not exactly what God had in mind, I'm sure, but God did honor my efforts. I began to renew my thoughts and think the thoughts of God instead of playing the old recordings of the past.

It was an effort all right. At first, it was strained and rehearsed when we talked. Then we started dating. Very quickly we were on the same page. We went to Guatemala with a couple bringing donated items to the poor. Then we went to Nicaragua with a pastor and saw God's hand on all of us to help the hurting. We also went to Costa Rica and were amazed at how happy we were together doing God's work.

About a month into the new thinking, I woke up, and

something stood out to me. I *loved* my husband. Yes, God had given that to me for my obedience. Obedience is truly better than sacrifice. The Bible says, "To obey is better than sacrifice" (1 Samuel 15:22). Doing what is right is better than suffering sacrificially to pay for what you've done. What an incredible realization and feeling. Actions will follow feelings, but don't expect feelings to dictate doing good all the time. Sometimes our emotions will deceive us into thinking we have to feel it first, and then we'll do it. That isn't what God says! He proves it again and again when we stand back years later being able to see where our emotions and feelings lied to us.

So how do you change your thoughts? Well, by simply thinking something else. "Sure, right!" you're saying. That's easier said than done.

Well, let's take a look at something you already know about. Have you ever told someone "I don't want to talk about it"? You have made a choice to think about something else for whatever reason. That's exactly how you change any of your other thoughts. At that point when you tell someone you don't want to talk about it, what happens next? You change the subject, right? You *do* already know how to change your thoughts. Now use this to make yourself a better, happier, and freer person. If you're capable of exercising your ability and choice to make the shift here, then you are fully capable of shifting in other situations too. It is a choice all the time.

Pretend you are talking just to yourself. I know there are times this is entirely true, as some of us argue back and forth with ourselves in our own minds. So if you were talking to someone else, you'd just tell them you don't want to go there. Why not tell that to yourself? Now what will you talk about to yourself?

Even the Psalmist in the Bible had issues in his life and spoke to himself. He asked himself, "Why are you downcast, O my soul? Why so disturbed within me? Put your hope in God, for I will yet praise him, my Savior and my God" (Psalm 42:5). I recall King David having many things to cast his soul down. He knew it was better not to dwell on those things but to remember the goodness of the Lord. He too had to change his natural thinking. The Bible says to renew your mind with God's word. But if you haven't chosen to let God rule your life, your mind may have a reflector that does not allow His message to penetrate. You could empty your mind, but all you'd have is empty space! How are you to gain anything from emptiness?

You must put something of value into your mind. There is no babble that you could just repeat over and over that is powerful enough to last. Sure, some people have talked themselves into a frenzy and think that is peace. I know sweet people who believe just speaking it will make it happen. What happens if it doesn't? Where are you putting your trust and security? Deep inside it becomes more difficult if you're left without hope. Hope must be present to go forward. Are you hoping in something worthy of your trust?

Do you want to grow forward and rethink your thoughts? What is your goal in rethinking? Is it to feel better, be better, live better? What is the reason we hope? I think this comes from a longing put in our hearts and minds to know our creator and purpose. Desiring purpose and meaning seems to be universal. A lot of thought and searching has been done throughout all of history to find the meaning of life. In simple terms, the meaning of life is to know God, to love Him, and to be loved by Him.

If there is no afterlife, what reason do we have to be better or kinder? Sure, it will be better for us here, but the mentality of first helping number one—yourself—would surely override goodness. It is not natural to think of someone else over yourself. There is a mindset with some people thinking there is a "survival of the fittest." That mindset would mean selfishness is better, eliminating the weakest, right? Wouldn't evolution operate under this method too? Evolutionary thinking should suggest that we strive for our own survival and none other. In thinking we have only evolved and there is no God, there would be no purpose of helping others. These are ways of thinking that do not change a world for the better. Selfish thinking does not make a person free. That is not how the rewards work in the natural law of God. Being better leads to feeling better, and being better also leads to living better. How do we become better? It starts with changing the way we think. We must think of others as well as ourselves. We must forgive and think differently toward our offenders. There is a spiritual law that is in effect as well.

Even if you are not a believer in Jesus, God's law, just like gravity, still exists. You don't get the full benefits available, but you will be able to use methods that work. It is like using battery operated power while you're here on earth. It may be strong enough for some things, but not all. Also, if you are not plugged into the true power source, your power will eventually die.

The following steps will benefit anyone who applies them, even if one isn't a believer in Jesus.

1. You must *say* that you will forgive your offender. You are not saying that they weren't guilty. Remember the snake? Release it!

2. Put yourself in the offender's place. Don't say, "I wouldn't have done that," but instead remember a time when you did something wrong to some one. Remember a time when someone accused you of offending them, and you denied it?

3. Make sure you haven't offended the person in question. You may ask them, but don't do it defensively. Do it to make things better. We can't always see clearly when we have been offended. Do not go to your offender telling them you forgive them unless they have asked for it. They may be defensive and justify what they have done. This will only make matters worse and could make you angrier.

4. Write the offense down on paper and deliberately make the physical motion to throw it away. Actions reinforce decision.

5. From now on, don't talk about that person negatively and treat the offender as though he/she never did anything. Maybe you are dealing with an offense that requires you to stay away from this person, such as a sexual offense. Then you must go through the forgiveness in your mind, but it does not require you to put yourself back in the situation again. If you see the person on the street, you continue to see yourself forgiving that person without letting them do it again.

6. If you are a believer in Jesus, you may tell Him you have full confidence that He is working through you to accomplish all good things. If you do not believe in Jesus, you will certainly have a harder time forgiving, but if you set your mind to do and accomplish it, then you will feel all the better for it. Life here on earth will be happier for you. It is your eternity that will suffer without Him.

Here is what the Bible says we are to do to our offenders.

> Be kind and compassionate to one another, forgiving each other, just as in Christ God forgave you. Bear with each other and forgive whatever grievances you may have against one another. Forgive as the LORD forgave you.
>
> Ephesians 4:32

> If it is possible, as far as it depends on you, live at peace with everyone. Do not take revenge, my friends, but leave room for God's wrath for it is written: "It is mine to avenge; I will repay," says the LORD. On the contrary: "If your enemy is hungry, feed him; if he thirsty, give him something to drink."
>
> Romans 12:18

Here is a very hard one, but we must realize that the hard sayings of the Bible are true!

> But love your enemies, do good to them and lend to them without expecting to get anything back. Then your reward will be great, and you will be sons of the Most High, because He is kind to the ungrateful and wicked. Be merciful, just as your Father is merciful.
>
> Luke 6:35–36

We must change our thoughts to those of God. He knows what is best and knows the outcome of each action. Forgiveness to some seems like having to give up something precious. What they don't realize is that it is akin to holding fool's gold thinking it is a treasure. At least the fool's gold is pretty to look at. Unforgiveness is not only worthless; it is a very ugly thing. We will reap what we sow. Maybe not at first, but like the crops that are planted that take time to have a harvest, so sometimes our efforts from sowing better things will require time. Do not become impatient with other people after you have followed those steps. It is you that is changing for the better. *They may never change. They don't have to for your change to take place. Your change will come when you change what you're thinking.*

I remember those times of difficulty with my husband. He would say things that were very destructive and insulting. These comments hurt me for years. Then I determined I was not going to let it happen again. Was I able to stop him from speaking? Of course not. But I, the receiver, was going to change *my* thoughts about what he said.

Most of the time we get hurt the most by those closest to us because we value their opinion the most. But that really doesn't determine *our* value. I asked God to change me. I believed that if I saw things differently I wouldn't be affected by words.

And so it happened. One day my husband said something hurtful in front of our adult daughter. She went off on him and then went off on me for "letting" him say those things. I honestly hadn't heard what he had said. The words not only lost the sting, but I actually did not even hear them. Wow! I wasn't hurt even after she told me what he had said. My thoughts were not linked to the evil any longer. My feelings toward my husband are still of love, and I care deeply for him. No need to fight when things don't matter. For me I had truly turned it all to the Lord. My value was in Him, and these comments wouldn't rule my actions or me. I was finally free! And years later, after insisting I would love my husband through it, realizing this was a false opinion he had of me, the comments came to an end. If we feed our minds with stuff other people throw on us, we go down with them. But if one changes the thoughts, the other has to eventually change, even if it is to simply give up. I can say now that my husband and I enjoy each other even though we don't agree all the time. Hey, I don't agree with myself sometimes. I am, however, free to live without the garbage slung on my back. Life is easier this way.

Changing your thoughts will definitely change your world. Just like wearing sunglasses cuts the glare and you see better, so forgiveness softens the glare of bitterness and allows us to see better. We have peace and freedom to see people as they really are, hurt most of the time. People react and live with hurt different ways, but I know we'd rather avoid it when we can. Forgiveness allows us to feel less pain rather than no forgiveness.

Change is difficult, but it is worth the effort. You can start now to change your thoughts. It is never too late to start. In fact, the longer you wait to do what is right after knowing, the harder it is to do it later. Smoking is an example. If you stop early it is easier than when you've done it for twenty years. If your mind has been cluttered with the garbage over the years, start with the one memory that hurts the worst and work your way through it all. But don't wait; get started now.

Exposing the Lies

You're not alone in your struggles. But again I say we have choices. One has to know the truth to know a lie. So I'm coming from the knowledge that the Bible is true. If you don't agree that the Bible is completely true, there will be many things we will disagree on. If you recognize some of these things as truth, then ask yourself if other things could be true as well. I want to expose some common lies that do not make our society better but keep people who believe these lies hurting and deceived. Many lies contribute to our holding unforgiveness as a whole, but even one of these lies can start a chain reaction of lifelong pain. Exposing these lies will help to get to the root of many reasons a person chooses unforgiveness.

One lie is that life does not begin at conception. If it doesn't, then when does it? When air hits the fetus? How is it that inside a woman it is a fetus and outside it is a baby? We know that inside an eagle egg is a baby eagle, and if anyone tampers with it, there is great penalty of law. How is it that we acknowledge the beginning of life in an egg but not in a woman? Yes, this book is about forgiveness, but it is also about life. My life was threatened simply on the basis of *how* I was conceived. Maybe this was because people are living with unforgiveness towards this kind of offender, even when they aren't personally involved. It is misguided unforgiveness and targeted at an innocent child. I am alive because my mother did not pass her offense on to me. I am alive because she realized I was a human and deserved a chance to live.

We are constantly fed lies about life. It starts with the lies that we are only a blob of tissue. We then struggle to find purpose. Girls in many public schools in the U.S. are taught that to have an abortion is okay because they aren't carrying a baby. It is only a blob of tissue. However, if a girl chooses to give birth and throw that same blob of tissue in a garbage can, she is prosecuted. I remember a woman who, hours before she was to deliver her baby, took a gun and shot herself in the abdomen. News reporters were appalled, but these same reporters thought abortion protestors were horrible.

The Bible says we *know* the truth but refuse it. Everyone seems to know it was wrong for those mothers mentioned above who destroyed those particular babies. This is hypocrisy on the part of the people (reporters), saying both that it *is* a baby and then in another situation that it *isn't* a baby. Either it is a baby or it isn't. People really do know the truth that it is a baby but choose a lie when most convenient. What makes the difference in these situations? The lie makes the difference. People know the truth but refuse to dwell on it for personal convenience.

So if we believe that life is not the result of the will of God, then we will not value life from the beginning. If a woman discovers that God is the originator of life after having had an abortion, then great remorse and bitterness takes hold of her. She may live with unforgiveness toward herself and anyone who helped her have that abortion, thus starting the chain of unforgiveness derived from lies.

Lying voices come into our minds sometimes as the voice of intellect. Society tells us that intelligence is very important, and our success is based on education, looks, and what we do. Satan has worked diligently to deceive us. We are taught to be proud, strong, and self-sufficient. Our own country founded on "independence"! If you need someone, you are perceived as weak. However, we readily follow "intellectuals" leading us astray. We believe in people who seem to have great wisdom in their findings, but these people seem to miss the obvious. Who are we really? What is our purpose? What is the meaning of all that we do? Those should be our questions.

Since we have also been fed lies about the beginning of life by intellectuals, some Christians are confused also. These lies have led to some Christians believing abortion is okay in the case of rape, deformity, or whatever isn't pleasant. Life is valuable, but we hear more and more that *quality* of life is the most important. Who qualifies to make this judgment? Who determines who lives or dies? Where is true compassion? This is pseudo-compassion seeking to rid society of the undesirables, the less than visually and physically perfect. Did I deserve the death penalty for the crime of my father? No! God said children are a blessing without exception.

What if Mary, the mother of Jesus, had aborted? She had all the reasons that today's society would use. Unwed, too young, an unwanted child coming into the world, shamed by society, but she had right thinking. She wanted the will of God in her life. Do you think it was easy for her? We are the recipients of her right thinking. *Who will be the recipient of your right thinking?*

The mother of Israel Houghton was thinking right

when she decided to keep her child. She was living in the Midwest with her family and became pregnant with her boyfriend's baby. Her boyfriend was black, and she was white. Her father gave her an ultimatum. Either she had an abortion, or he would disown her. She refused to abort. He did disown her, but she stood by her decision. Even when the father of her baby did not stay with her, Israel's mother chose to keep her child. She moved to California and, when Israel was about one year old, married a man who would love Israel as his own. Today Israel, having won many Dove, Stellar, and Grammy awards, is blessing millions with his powerful praise and dedication to serving God. He is married and has three talented children of his own. This man could have chosen a bitter life keeping racial insults and other offenses, but he pressed through to reap a harvest of great blessings.

James Robison, from Life Today Ministries, is another person conceived in rape and making a difference in our world. Rebecca Kiessling is a lawyer speaking up for the life of the unborn because she too was conceived in rape. Bethaney Tessitore, another life conceived in rape, is an opthamologist giving back and making a difference as she also takes her gifts around the world.

If you have a passion to be free, I challenge you to seek truth for yourself and do as author and investigative reporter Lee Stroebel did for himself. While many want to say there are contradictions in the Bible, those same people rarely have researched to prove that point. However, this man, Lee Stroebel spent two years trying to *disprove* the Bible, coming away convinced of its authenticity and truth. He has written several books on his findings. The Bible says there is no temptation that is not common to man. The temptation to believe a lie is common but can be exposed by the truth and rejected.

While we sit alone with our thoughts, we are convinced we are the only ones going through a situation. "Why me?" has been asked by every human able to process thoughts. Does evolution ask why? It doesn't seem a question like this is needed if you are just evolving, right? It should be accepted as part of the process. Thoughts like that don't come from evolving. I make mention of evolution again for the purpose of debunking the idea. It is free will, the gift of God, that allows us to even question life and Him! We have been fed lies that we have evolved, and people accept that as fact without seeking truth. It doesn't matter that evidence does *not* exist to support Darwin's evolution *theory;* people hold on to those lies unto death. If we think we are just here by chance and life ends here on earth, what real drive will we have to better ourselves? We will only perpetuate the "look out for #one" thinking. Unforgiveness is a viable choice if there are no lasting consequences, as evolution would dictate. But no matter how slow they seem to occur, consequences will happen.

Some people will stay in a burning building and die because they don't believe they will jump into the safety of the firemen's net below. We look at this and say what a shame. What would make a person not take a lesser risk to possibly save their life? Lies are the reason. The mind has traded the truth for a lie. The result is always the same. *Death!* Oh, we don't always see that extreme demonstration, but that is where it eventually leads. Death of a relationship, our hopes for the future, our life's potential. Remember the domino effect? This also happens when we live with the lies.

Let's take abuse for example. My adopted mother was abused, so she abused. Some people believe the lie of "That's just the way I am and the way it's been for generations. I can't change who I am!" I had the choice to come away feeling I deserve to be abused or to be an abuser. While I didn't choose either of those, I did come away believing I wasn't much of anything. These are *lies* I chose to believe. These lies affected every aspect of my life—my relationships with loved ones, my confidence to accomplish things, and my relationship with God.

When we think *how could God let this happen,* we are thinking from our own viewpoint and circumstances, missing the potential God has given us. He sees things so differently from us. When we finally see things His way, it is a wonderful experience. People wonder why it took them so long to believe. I wonder why I ever chose lies over His truth.

Living with the lies of being inadequate made me a people pleaser but also strong willed. While the strong will part of me acted out, sometimes I allowed men to take advantage of me. Satan took the molestation and used it to create lies about me and my relationships. Many people live with the lies of inferiority passed on by offenders.

When children are hurt, through molestation for instance, lies will fill their mind. Lies of worthlessness and deserving what happened seem to make no sense to people on the outside, but it is very real to the victim. Lives of promiscuity seem to come out of this sort of abuse. When we realize our worth to God, then lies that come from being hurt disappear, and forgiveness for ourselves and our offenders is possible.

Women and men both fall for these lies. Young men who have been raped by a man can easily start believing they are homosexual. I have met them. A girl can believe that sex is all she is good for. Lies such as "I am not worthy of love" and "I have to do anything to keep a man's affection and attention" were ever present in my young life. This way of thinking never works and certainly does not bring happiness.

People sell out, not hearing the voice of God calling out with His true love. Jealousy, ulcers, depression, divorce, prostitution, drug use—the list goes on and on of what happens to people when they listen to the lies and hold unforgiveness. The truth is that listening to those lies can kill you. Uncontrollable illness can occur. Also thoughts of suicide can lead to following through.

Why do people commit suicide? We know it is because they traded the truth for a lie. They believe life isn't worth living and that their life has no value or hope. We stand back and can see that wasn't true. It's never a fast decision for most people who commit suicide. They have played those thoughts over and over in their minds. Not forgiving ourselves can also lead to feelings of worthlessness and hopelessness.

I distinctly recall suicidal thoughts on three occasions. The first was at thirteen years old after believing I "couldn't take it anymore." The second time was when I was thirty-two years old, married and feeling unloved. And the third time was at forty-eight years old, when I was told I was conceived in rape, and the voices of worthlessness and hopelessness came again.

On that second occasion of suicidal thoughts, I stood with a knife in my hand, cutting chicken for dinner. Hurt and angry, I was thinking once again that my life wasn't worth living. At this point in my life, I had been a born again believer in Christ for about three years. I was still struggling with self-worth because I hadn't really grasped the love of God or who I was in Him. So it is with other believers not living in the power available to them. The devil's strongholds are still intact. I believed the lie that there was no hope. That is really what kills us. To think there is no hope means there can be no change and no future. But the Bible tells us in Jeremiah 29:11 that God gives us a future and a hope.

As I stood with that knife in my hand that day, something extremely strange happened. I saw a vision of myself lying in a pool of blood after stabbing myself. Then I heard a voice say, "*Do it!*" But as plainly as I heard that voice, another said, "No!" Just then it was like an invisible hand grabbed my hand and sent the knife flying across the room. It hit a picture in the wall, taking a chunk out of the frame. Was I crazy? No, I know angels intervened for my safety. The Bible tells us that God has given angels charge over us. I not only believed it I saw it. I am glad that the lie was exposed and I didn't follow through with my original thoughts.

I too lived with the lies that affected my life and those around me. It wasn't until I knew the person I am in Christ that my life really took a drastic change for the better. Sure I was slowly getting better anyway, but knowing who I am was no comparison to not knowing. I didn't just get better—I was completely changed! It is the difference between dark and light.

Lies can come from other people telling them to us or from our own thoughts. We all hear voices in our head.

Some are our own, and others are from an enemy seeking to destroy us. For me, the voices of destruction in my head may have been louder because I was adopted. The feeling of loss was there even though I had loving parents. What I didn't know growing up was that almost everyone feels worthless and rejected at some point in his or her life. The voices begin early. Even as children we hear, *"You're ugly; no one likes you; you're dumb."* If you're the popular one, sometimes the thoughts creep in that people really don't like you, that you're not smart enough, or that someone will take your place. The recording never stops. We fight those voices till the day we die. Some people are plagued with voices that they cannot ignore, and thus we send them off to institutions.

Why do some people find it impossible to make the voices stop? I believe that power comes from only one source. Coming from the point of view that God created everything, I believe He is capable of controlling everything. Sure, we can have methods and medicine that will help. Ultimately, God alone can fix something perfectly and permanently. Therefore we can go to Him with these problems and expect that He will help us. We must surrender every part of our lives to God. Next, believe and expect; then we will see God work with us. Forgiveness will make the voices powerless. The voices may be there, but through God we have control over them.

Some people believe the lie that God doesn't talk to us. Perhaps you even think a thought sometimes that you dismiss as your own. There is a voice we hear that is the voice of God guiding us to do what is right. We cannot take ownership of that voice, nor should we ignore it. Some just brush it off as conscience, but where does that come from? We all know that inkling to do something or to not do it. Maybe we have an urge to go to a certain place and don't know why. What about the sick feeling you get when you are about to do something wrong? That *is* the voice of conscience, which *is* the voice of God. The more we push that away, the softer it gets until we no longer hear it. Like the candle that goes out for lack of oxygen, so too the voice of God will fade for lack of attention.

If you feel you have not heard the voice of God, ask Him to speak to you. Trust that He will. The Bible says our consciences are seared after repeated rejection of God's voice and truth. Do not reject His truth, and you *will* hear Him. Become "His people" through Christ, and you are guaranteed to hear from Him.

We can choose to be happy—is this a truth or a lie? A counselor once told me that we choose to be happy. What? My mind couldn't grasp this concept in the midst of pain. Was he crazy? Had he not ever experienced pain? In fact, I was in such pain that I asked him, "So, if I slap you across the face right now, you would still be happy?" He just stared at me without replying. And I thought, *I guess he wouldn't!*

Now looking back I suppose he knew I was unable or just refusing to believe there was a choice, so he chose to remain silent. He knew I wasn't going to believe anything he attempted to tell me. I understand now that I will always have a choice to think as I wish. I will act on what I think, and I will become what I have been dwelling on. Happiness is in the moment, and we can't always *feel* that happiness. But a better way is through joy. Joy is something that is deep within and is sustained through the bad times. Joy takes over when happiness is gone, because joy comes from God. Happiness is a temporary fix that is man made. I can choose to have joy in all circumstances because happy lasts for a while but joy will last always. Joy will allow us to forgive, but happiness is always needy.

There are lies about responsibility. This lie leaves us believing someone else "made" us unhappy or angry or bitter. But the truth is that no one can make you that way. You must choose it for yourself! As I have gone through life, I have experienced firsthand the power of my own thinking. Life and death are in the power of the tongue, as Proverbs 18:21 says that power comes first from what we think. We can destroy others and ourselves with what we say but *only* if the receiver believes. No one can be destroyed unless they allow it. (I am not talking about the physical.)

If you think long enough, you will start to believe it, whatever you are thinking. Believing truth is the key to life where forgiveness is the door. Believing truth will lead you to forgiveness and then ultimate freedom.

Thinking truth occasionally is not good enough. A lie can destroy us at any level. Thinking and dwelling on truth will bring new life every day.

Thinking is our fuel for life. It can give energy to live or be the poison that kills. Lies will be the shifting sands that the Bible talks about. Just as a house cannot stand on shifting sands, so our lives cannot survive the shifting between lies and truth. We must live in truth to live in fullness of life.

Lies will grow stronger with each embrace. We first begin by embracing it, and then the end comes when the lie takes hold of us with its death grip. Lies come at us in subtle ways, slipping in unnoticed. If they make a bold, abrupt entrance, we can usually see them. So evil has a very sophisticated and quite successful method of infiltration. Mixing truth with the lie makes it more acceptable, easing into even the critic's heart. The Bibles tells us to "watch and pray so that you will not fall into temptation. The spirit is willing but the body is weak" (Mark 14:38). We must be on guard not to fall for the lies and thus fall into temptation.

In the Garden of Eden, lies began mixed with truth. Satan said that in the day that they would eat the fruit, they would be like God. God had said if they ate the fruit, they would die (be separated from Him). Then Satan twisted it to make God look bad. He wanted Eve to think God just didn't want them to be like God. It is not unlike today when people feel God doesn't want them to have fun with all His rules. He really just wants to spare us from knowing *evil*. The fruit would let Adam and Eve know good and evil. They *already* knew the purity of good. So all that was left was to know evil.

Eve chose to focus on the part that would make her be like God. She thought this would make her happy. She traded the lie of happiness *as* God for the joy of being *with* God. In doing so she missed the rest of the trap. She was going to know evil. With her disobedience her eyes would see clearly the evil she had done. She and Adam would know firsthand the definition of evil. While they were in the moment, they concentrated on the activity or their goal, not the consequences. There will come a day when all we have done will be exposed. *All* lies will be exposed. Our own relative truths will not be sufficient on the day we die. There is a way that seems right but only leads to destruction. Scripture says it twice, first in Proverbs 14:12 and then in 16:25. So Eve led Adam the wrong way. How often do we listen to voices in our heads telling us to go the wrong way? Or go along with someone else provoking us to do something we know is wrong?

Have you ever tried to forgive someone and have a "friend" tell you not to? Sometimes those voices and other people play with our emotions to convince us they know what's best. Beware—that voice that convinced you to do wrong will be the same voice to condemn you once you go through with it.

Ever done something wrong, even as a Christian, and then heard something tell you how horrible you were and that you will never be forgiven for what you've done? This is another lie. *It is best to know what God says at all times for the maximum living experience!*

We are also afraid of rejection. We follow the persuasion of those that try to get us to do wrong, lying to ourselves that we need that person's approval to survive. Or we go the opposite way and refuse any help from anyone. If we do it ourselves, we think we will escape the hurt someone else could inflict on us. We miss so much by doing this and actually hurt ourselves either way.

A great quote that most of us already know is by Alfred Lord Tennyson: "'Tis better to have loved and lost than never to have loved at all."[2] Still another quote worth mentioning is by Washington Irving: "Love is never lost. If not reciprocated, it will flow back and soften and purify the heart."[3]

I tend to agree with him but only if we *allow* our hearts to be purified. God is love, and only God can purify our hearts. Left to itself, the heart can grow cold and stone-like. We can learn, however, so much from loving without counting the risk. Forgiveness is like this too, because I believe forgiveness is the greatest act of love. Jesus did it when He went to the cross and forgave us of all our sins.

We have accepted lies about our lack of the need for God and each other. These two things we need to be whole and achieve love and forgiveness, for ourselves and for others. The scripture says to even love your enemy. We need each other. We *need* God!

Have you heard the lie, "Live for yourself"? The will of the Lord is the only thing worth living for, and since we are created by Him for Him, why would we think we could actually live free apart from Him? When we are focused on His will, wow, what a difference it makes; we *will* do all things because He strengthens us. Plus the added bonus of unspeakable joy comes when we do the right thing.

Many people look at Christians and religion as a crutch and have accepted the lies that a person needs no one to survive. *Lies!* We all need one another, and I dare say that without God giving to us our very breath, we are miserably helpless and hopeless.

If we have an enemy that wants to destroy us, why wouldn't that enemy start with lying about our value? Certainly if he were able to convince people that there was no value or purpose, surely he could use those same people to destroy the ones that did value life. What if we could be convinced that life doesn't start at conception? More people could be destroyed early. And if they weren't destroyed early, he would never give up working on their thoughts. That is where he wins the war. It is in the deception.

We hear statements like, "We must take care of ourselves because no one else will," and "This is the only life we have, so live it up now." Also we are told that we can do whatever we want today, for tomorrow we die and there is nothing else. These are all lies. There is evidence all around that proves we are designed and not made in chaos. Does anything you know form a complex, intricately functioning machine when you bomb something? No, never has; never will. This is obvious, but people have replaced the truth with a lie.

Subtleties slip into our society to take God out. Things such as the changes that are being made in our history are increasing. Using Thomas Jefferson's letter to a woman to keep religion out of our government is opposite of what was intended. The following is taken from his letter exactly.

> Believing with you that religion is a matter which lies solely between Man & his God, that he owes account to none other for his faith or his worship, that the legitimate powers of government reach actions only, & not opinions, I contemplate with sovereign reverence that act of the whole American people which declared that their legislature should "make no law respecting an establishment of religion, or prohibiting the free exercise thereof," thus building a wall of separation between Church & State. [4]

It was intended to keep government from getting into "church" business and to protect churches against the government, not the other way around. The original history and formation of our country was entirely God centered. Schools do not teach this and in fact will try to remove the freedom to speak about God. We are becoming less free. The exclusion of God in our country will *not* make us free.

The older people remember how it was, but we are conditioned to not respect or value older people. But age doesn't gain the respect it once did. We hate the idea of growing old because we are told that youthful strength and beauty in the physical is far more valuable than wisdom of the aged. We have been told old is worthless and burdensome. *Lies!* This thought makes it easy to form bitterness for something said in truth. The older people tend to "say it like it is." Some people younger than these will become offended by the truth they speak. They are dismissed as old and "not in the know." Unforgiveness in this way will block learning from the aged. Remember, Satan does not want us to know truth in any way.

Old ways make way for newer nonrestrictive ways. "If it feels good, do it" has been a saying for many years. So our society puts away the important things for instant gratification of the flesh. Forgiveness doesn't usually bring instant gratification, so we sometimes fall for the lie that forgiveness is unattainable. The older people suffer, and so does everyone else. Many now think euthanasia is a great and compassionate thing. Who has the right to be God, or at the very least the ruler of life and death over another? Much can be learned from our older people, but too many waste away in nursing homes for convenience of their children. Perhaps lack of forgiveness is one of the reasons children use to justify their actions. The Bible says to honor our father and mother, but it does not say only if they have been good to us. There are blessings that come with that command. Peace is one of them. I know a woman who was raped by her father when she was young, yet she lives with forgiveness and is taking care of him in his old age.

It is easy to turn away and justify ourselves. That justification is a lie to keep us from our blessings. It isn't easy to do what is right, but as we do it and expose the lies, it does become easier.

Let me say that I realize there are some older people who actually like their living arrangements. There are also those older people requiring professional care that benefit greatly from being in an environment capable of taking care of them. I am not referring to those people. Far too many people don't need to be in nursing homes. They are put away and forgotten, their wisdom wasting away. Some people live with the lie that the older people are responsible for all the trouble in the world, thus justifying unforgiveness, which leads to neglect. Exposing these lies will also expose unforgiveness.

Unforgiveness shows up in so many areas of our lives, and lies cover up truth. We must know that the unforgiveness is in our hearts before we can deal with it. *Usually we will find it hidden under a lie!* I have talked to many people who are sorry once their parents have died. Left with remorse but without resolution, these people feel they no longer have the ability to forgive even the living. Some may take that unforgiveness to their own graves. This is not necessary. Forgiveness happens on the side of the forgiver first. The truth is that forgiveness can be done at any time, and it only requires one person, not two or more.

Even though lies may have filled our minds, we can expose them and then take action.

Lie exposed: Do not accept anything from an offender—advice, restitution, kindness. People are deceived into throwing away all that an offender says based on one failure in their past. What if that person has learned a great and valuable lesson and wants to pass it on? Forgiveness allows us to move freely and to be open to learning.

Years of experience will show over and over the tactics of our spiritual enemy. Unforgiveness can be carried for generations. People or cultures whose families were offended years ago may still hold bitterness today towards the descendents of the original offenders. Lie exposed: we must hold generations accountable for the original crime. This keeps the offense, as well as unforgiveness, fresh. Lies keep bitterness active. Can you see how subtle lies affect a whole society? There are groups of people who won't work together for the good of mankind because they hold offenses from generations past.

Having spoken with the persecuted Christians worldwide through Voice of the Martyrs, I have found in them joy unspeakable. How could that be, you ask? They have known the depths of pain but heights of joy in the embrace of their Savior, Jesus Christ. They trusted, believed, and thought on how Jesus truly loved them. They keep their focus on their future with Him. Voice of the Martyrs is a foundation dedicated to helping Christians who are persecuted for their faith. Over and over their reports feature people from many different parts of the world living in forgiveness towards their attackers. These people must seem strange at first. It is not natural to show love and forgiveness to those who offend us. How much more unnatural is it to show forgiveness to someone who wants you dead? It is not impossible, as these Christians are proving with their own actions.

Jeremiah 29:11 tells us that God thinks good thoughts toward us, and he wants to give us a future and a hope. Opportunity in suffering becomes great, opportunity for learning great secrets of life, strengthening hopes, and being the glory of the Almighty God.

These are the things I have chosen to think on and believe. These are the things that truly lift me up when I am feeling like I am at my lowest. I know who I am and who loves me—my creator, my God, my Jesus.

———

Do you feel like I have, depressed and down for no known reason? You can't even explain why. Where did *that* come from? If you met me you would see that I am a very upbeat, energetic person. Most of the time, I am very happy. There may be a battle that almost seems insurmountable, but I turn to the Lord.

Everyday a battle rages for our souls. Even I must fight the battle with conscious effort, or I too will be kept from my purpose and destiny. Many people are wounded and have a reason for depression, and that makes things so much more difficult. That is truth.

If we have Jesus as our Lord *and* Savior, much is available to us. No matter if we are hurt or just feeling depressed for no reason, we must rise up to proclaim who we are in Christ. Without the power of Jesus, we are struggling in a giant ocean without anything to cling to. We eventually go down to the depths of darkness. We have an enemy that has a mission to take us down and out. Truth says that there is one that is greater than that. Lie exposed: others are the cause of our unhappiness. More lies tell us they don't deserve our forgiveness.

One excuse for not choosing to believe the word of God is because people look at other people to be God for them. Yes, people have distorted God's word to force their way. Just go back to the truth. Read what Jesus said concerning the love of our enemies. We are to watch Him as an example and keep our eyes off people to save us.

You also have the choice to change because God said, "Today I set before you life and death. Choose life!" I used to wonder why He had to tell us to choose life. Wasn't it obvious? I guess not because most of us have chosen death in our thinking on more than one occasion. It would be great if we were like computers—just put in another CD. But God has given us His word to replace the word of the enemy. If we use His word, it truly does change our thinking. Think on the truth and expose the lies.

Truth is, we must stop having conversations with the enemy. Jesus only used scripture to reply to him. Can you hear yourself agreeing with the enemy sometimes? Lie exposed: "You can't do anything; don't even try," and you say, "Yeah, I remember the time I failed, and I will probably fail again." *Stop it!* That is the foundation for death. Choose life and don't waste any time. Please do it now because you really do have an assignment to glorify God here should you *choose* to pursue it.

Lies about what fixes things in our life are rampant.

Some seek medication while others drown themselves in work. Others rebel against a world of hurt. Do these things make it better? Perhaps if you have a chemical imbalance, medication will help. My question is this: can God heal everyone? I realize that for some reason, some are not healed, and only God has the answer for that. But why wouldn't we ask anyway and trust that He *will?* Too many of us automatically run to doctors, lawyers, and anyone else except God to fix our problems. The Bible says that anything done lacking faith is unpleasing to God. I know that one hurts because I have felt the sting of "lack of faith." God shows a solution for even that problem. A man asked Jesus, "I believe. Help me with my unbelief." So there is still hope for the doubting. Lie exposed: we are hopeless. *We are never hopeless with Jesus.* Even the great people of the Bible talked to themselves to achieve right thinking. David asked his own soul why it was cast down. Lots of people chant things to get their minds into focus. Faith comes by hearing, hearing by the word of God. Even if your ears have to hear your own mouth speak God's word to you, speak loudly and clearly.

Another lie is that unforgiveness is acceptable. The truth is that our natural feeling is to hate our enemy. But that is another lie that keeps the world from knowing peace. Truth is the concept of loving your enemy is found only in the Bible. If that makes no sense to you, I ask you to just trust God and put it into practice anyway. I've seen it work countless times. Peace that passes all understanding *does* come with forgiveness. It may take some time to see results. Give yourself that time. Although some people have seen instant change, others do not. This does not mean there is no God or that you really haven't forgiven. There are different recipes for bread that require different temperatures and different times, but that doesn't mean some are not bread. If you have given your life to Christ, you *are* a child of God. You must trust God at His word, no matter what life looks like around you. He has a specific plan for your life, and it requires something just right for you. That's patience again. We would do well to learn how valuable patience is. Great lessons are learned as we walk in patience. Lie exposed: we need all our desires instantly fulfilled.

Lie exposed: when we do what is right, everything will be right around us. It seems that when we are determined to do what is right, the opportunity to be tested is everywhere. Lies will fill your mind as many times as possible. They will try to convince you nothing is working, so you may as well give up. You must believe you will never regret doing what is right, *never!* If you dwell on lying thoughts, you will be sucked in and act upon them. *Truth is, if doing the right thing were so easy, there'd be no laws to keep us in line.*

It will always be a struggle, but as we continue to do right, it will become easier. Have I reached a point with no struggles to say the right thing or think the right thing? *No!* But I find it easier than it was twenty years ago. So do not be discouraged.

As I am writing this I am given ample opportunity to exercise forgiveness. Even within my own family, there is a struggle to break through barriers. Little things get bigger and bigger, making it a very difficult and discouraging time. Please know this is normal. Even Paul wrote in the Bible that each time he wanted to do good, evil was right there with him. We must live in a state of constant forgiveness to have that perfect peace within ourselves.

Satan doesn't want to lose his grip and thus allow us to succeed with God. He will even use unsuspecting Christians, the ones closest to us, to hurt us the most. Just keep doing what is right. Even if it looks like you will lose everything, don't be swayed.

I actually had someone that I love dearly tell me, "I don't want to be your friend." That was one of the hardest things, if not the hardest thing, I have ever heard. I couldn't have hurt more if that person would have stabbed me in my heart with a knife. Loved ones can hurt us the most because we care about them the most. This person sees nothing wrong with that statement. So I must choose to forgive and continue loving without reservation. Is that hard? You bet it is. I feel rejected, which causes me to fear I will be hurt again. So my first instinct is to run away. God does not want us to run away. Lie exposed: Christians will be exempt from other Christians hurting them. People will make mistakes knowingly or not, and we will probably hurt others too.

I will, however, respect this person's wishes. Our relationship will not develop past where that person allows. If there is someone in your life like this, continue to pray love and understanding for them. Pray that the enemy be bound so that God's love can rule. Do not avoid that person entirely but be led by the Lord as to what to do. Lie exposed: I can give an offender the cold shoulder. The truth is that Jesus instructed us to love our enemies. So we can certainly love (doing good toward) someone who is less than our enemy.

Some older parents have children who are distant, but

God will guide you as you continue to pray. We are called to be accountable for our own actions. If I have offended someone, I want to be quick to ask forgiveness. Also, for those who have offended me, I want to be quick to forgive. Lie exposed: I don't have to forgive anyone who doesn't ask for it. Jesus forgave us even when we were sinners and didn't know him. We may even be hit with daily tests requiring forgiveness. Relationships should be an example of the love God has for us.

Lie exposed: if I forgive, there will be no more tension. To move into the zone of doing right may result in feeling tense or awkward. Tension means evil isn't happy. It is easy to fall or slip into doing wrong. You must plan to do right! Think about the things that will enable you to do what's right. Imagine yourself in a situation before it happens. What will you say or do when you see your offender face to face? Don't be caught off guard.

Here is a quick list of common lies along with the truth: *Nothing will change.*

> Everything is possible for him who believes.
>
> > Mark 9:23

I don't have to take that anymore.

> Jesus told Peter to forgive seventy times seventy.

> Consider it pure joy, my brothers whenever you face trials of many kinds, because you know that the testing of your faith develops perseverance. Perseverance must finish its work so that you may be mature and complete, not lacking anything.
>
> > James 1:2

Then Peter came to Jesus and asked

"LORD, how many time shall I forgive my brother when he sins against me? Up to seven times?" Jesus answered, "I tell you, not seven times, but seventy times seven."

Matthew 18–21–22

I need to look after only myself.

…but in humility consider others better than yourself.

Philippians 2:3

I need to get more than I give.

more blessed to give than to receive.

Acts 20:35

Getting even will make me feel better.

It is mine to avenge. I will repay.

Deuteronomy 32:35

Do not repay evil with evil or insult with insult, because to this you were called so that you may inherit a blessing.

1 Peter 3:9

I can't forgive myself.

When Jesus saw their faith he said, "Friend your sins are forgiven."

1 John 1:9

If we confess our sins He is faithful and just and will forgive us our sins and purify us from all unrighteousness.

Luke 5:20

Wealth is the most important thing in life.

What good is it for a man to gain the whole world, and yet lose or forfeit his very self?

Luke 9:25

Looks and abilities determine human value.

The LORD does not look at the things man looks at. Man looks at the outward appearance, but the LORD looks at the heart.

1 Samuel 16:7

Being old is worthless.

God can use older people in mighty ways. Sarah had doubts, but she did have a child in her old age.

Abraham and Sarah were already old and well advanced in years, and Sarah was past the age of childbearing. So Sarah laughed to herself as she thought,

"After I am worn out and my master is old, will I now have this pleasure."

Genesis 18:11–12

And she added,

"Who would have said to Abraham that Sarah would nurse children? Yet I have borne him a son in his old age"

Genesis 21:7

I said, Age should speak, and advanced years should teach wisdom

Job 32:7

They shall still bring forth fruit in old age ...

Psalms 92:14

Evolution is no longer a theory but is now fact.

There is a way that seems right to a man, but in the end it leads to death.

Proverbs 14:12

In the beginning God created the heavens and the earth.

Genesis 1:1

There is no God, and there are no consequences after we die.

Just as man is destined to die once, and after that to face judgment.

Hebrews 9:27

History doesn't matter.

I want you to recall the words spoken in the past by the holy prophets and the command given by our LORD and Savior through your apostles.

Deuteronomy 4:9

Only be careful, and watch yourselves closely so that you do not forget the things your eyes have seen or let them slip from your heart as long as you live. Teach them to your children and to their children after them.

2 Peter 3:2

Parents are of no value to adult children.

> Honor your father and mother, so that you may live long.
>
> Exodus 20:12

Truth is relative and changes with each person.

> There is a way that seems right to a man, but in the end it leads to death.
>
> Proverbs 16:25

Life does not begin at conception.

> Before I formed you in the womb I knew you, before you were born I set you apart.
>
> Jeremiah 1:5

Abortion does not kill a human baby.

> While Jesus tells us it is no longer required to take a life for a life, this verse shows the importance of the life of the unborn.
>
> If men who are fighting hit a pregnant woman and she gives birth prematurely but there is no serious injury, the offender must be fined whatever the woman's husband demands and the court allows. But if there is serious injury, you are to take life for life.
>
> Exodus 21:22–23

Euthanasia is humane and compassionate.

> Don't you know that you yourselves are God's temple and that God's Spirit lives in you.
>
> 1 Corinthians 3:16

We also know the commandment, do not kill.

It is better to destroy a baby than to give it to someone who wants one. Rape babies don't deserve to live. (This means I didn't deserve to live!)

…children a reward from him.

Psalm 127:3

Now if you are not being affected by those lies, the devil will try a different approach.

Oh, you're not that bad. At least you don't do _____!

If we say that we have no sin, we deceive ourselves, and the truth is not in us.

1 John 1:8

You have the right to be angry and get even.

But God says: It is mine to avenge. I will repay. Do not repay evil with evil or insult with insult, because to this you were called so that you may inherit a blessing.

1 Peter 3:9

It is mine to avenge; I will repay.

Deuteronomy 32:35

God wants you to be happy, so you can do anything.

Consecrate yourselves therefore and be holy, because I am holy.

Leviticus 11:44

Churches are full of hypocrites.

> For all have sinned and fall short of the glory of God.
>
> Psalm 4:5

> Offer right sacrifices and trust in the LORD.
>
> Romans 3:23

God knows my heart, and though I am in this sin, he understands I am just weak.

> Do not be deceived: God cannot be mocked. A man reaps what he sows.
>
> Galatians 6:7

People are too judgmental, and I don't have to listen to them.

> If anyone thinks he is something when he is nothing he deceives himself. Each one should test his own actions.
>
> Galatians 6:3

I don't have to read my Bible to be a good Christian.

> Do not add to what I command you and do not subtract from it, but keep the commands of the LORD your God that I give you.
>
> 2 Timothy 2:15

> Do your best to present yourself to God as one approved, a workman who does not need to be ashamed and who correctly handles the word of truth.
>
> Deuteronomy 4:2

I can hide this sin, and no one will get hurt.

> "Wait till the LORD comes. He will bring to light what is hidden in darkness and will expose the motives of men's hearts"
>
> 1 Corinthians 4:5

I can't control myself.

> But the fruit of the Spirit is love, joy, peace, patience, kindness, goodness, faithfulness, gentleness and *self-control.* (emphasis added)
>
> Galatians 5:22

The list could go on and on, but can you see how just believing *one* of these lies can change the world. Resources at the end of the book will allow you to take the easy road to searching. Walk where others have done the work for you. Free yourself to believe truth and see a whole new world come alive. If you *are* a believer, these resources will strengthen your beliefs.

Why do people choose a lie? Immediate gratification is one reason. We don't want to suffer any consequences, so the brain will put it off as long as possible, pretending the consequences don't exist. Thinking we can escape altogether is another reason to believe the lie. Perhaps we are the few, the lucky, that will escape the consequences because we are different or special. Ever think, "That won't happen to me. It only happens to other people?" Then something happens and blows that theory.

Lies enable us to change reality to our benefit, or so we think. The truth about God is one that does not come easy because we fight to make ourselves answer to only ourselves. So for those who choose Christianity, we must relinquish our whole life to God, who we have not seen or touched for ourselves. He has left His Bible and instructions for life, but somehow we think we can do better. If we think we can do better on our own, then we have another reason for choosing unforgiveness.

Christianity is the only religion with a risen savior that was visible to over five hundred people. He was seen going up into the sky saying he would return. Who will we believe?

And what if this is all true? What happens to those who chose not to believe? I asked that to someone, and their reply was, "I'll just take my chances!" That is a gamble of the highest stakes—life!

Do not gamble your life away living lies. One lie is that unforgiveness is acceptable. The root, however, is really in not taking God at his word. God is life. Life and death are choices. Every choice you make will be on one side or the other. There is *no* middle ground. Choose life, choose truth, and choose forgiveness, because God is real!

Justification or Forgiveness

First, you must see truth to make right choices. Whether you understand or not, truth is always right.

People who believe they are "good" persons and justify themselves by the good things they do are in denial of the evil that is present in them too. We all know we are not perfect, but not all want to find a solution to that problem. Even if a person believes they are a victim, justified in unforgiveness, truth is not seen, and peace will not come. There is no middle ground. Forgiveness is necessary on both sides.

Denial does not make truth no matter how many times we say something doesn't exist. If we have lied, stolen, or spoken badly about someone, we are liars, thieves, and gossips. Have you turned away from those things? Who hasn't done just one of these three things? So how was that punished? Did we really get off the hook? Who is perfect to correct these imperfections? No one is perfect, and everyone can say that. But to say people need a savior becomes very difficult and even provokes anger in some people. Why? Because there are consequences we know we deserve.

People become nervous when confronted with sin. Oh, even the word is taboo. But sin is disobedience to God's moral law. Yes, *God's* moral law. I ask the question, did evolution come up with morals? Doesn't evolution believe in survival of the fittest? Then the answer would be no. We cannot justify ourselves when deep inside we know what is wrong.

While you are trying to live in denial, your conscience can be immobilized or paralyzed. Little by little things are done to whittle away at any feeling of wrong. Dwelling on lies also keeps the conscience from being active. *The longer a person justifies himself, the harder it is to see the truth.* Layers of deceit suffocate the knowledge of the truth.

People try to justify their wrong while condemning the exact same thing in another. I saw a man zipping through traffic cutting everyone off one day. Then a car cut in front of him. That man, who was now the one being wronged, *saw* that it was wrong when it was done to him. He was outraged. Proof that he knew right from wrong!

We will be accountable for all our actions one day. But will we be able to justify ourselves? No.

Ever try to make an excuse for yourself in a situation like being late for lunch with a friend? You lie and say something about the traffic, knowing you just left later than you should because you wanted to get something else done. You want to be justified and get off the hook. The person you are having lunch with will not know the truth because they can't see all things. But God can. So when we approach Him when we die, He will "see right through us." There will be no excuses and no justification.

People make up all sorts of reasons for the way they feel or live. Some believe they have the right to do wrong because of their upbringing, their income level, or how much they have been hurt. *There is no excuse for any wrongdoing.* People who make excuses for their wrongs because of someone else's wrongs are living with unforgiveness. They end up no better than their offender.

Don't you just hate when people make excuses to you for doing something wrong? Why? We were made in the likeness of God. We get upset because He gets upset with this kind of behavior.

Again, I bring up evolution to ask: can we look to evolution for the answer? Do evolutionists applaud deceit because we have no purpose and are just randomly made? I repeat myself to say "survival of the fittest" should keep us striving to succeed over the weak minded and vulnerable. We say we believe in survival of the fittest. But we do not applaud such behavior, and we know it is wrong when it is done to us. We live a double standard and thus know truth, but we justify ourselves in not living by it. We want forgiveness when *we* do something wrong but are not so quick to deliver it to our offenders. If evolution was true, wouldn't we all be justified in retaliating to succeed? My point is to show we know right from wrong. Evolution is another lie to keep us from living with respect and value of life. Thus making it easier to perpetuate unforgiveness.

I am against evolution, as you probably can tell by now. Evolution would say that my life or even yours is just a random happening. When we understand how valuable each life is, we become alive. It will become increasingly difficult to justify ourselves with lies if we truly value others and forgive them.

So if we cannot justify ourselves for our wrongdoing, then what? We cannot hold unforgiveness towards others either, thinking we are justified. We need someone to save *us*. God thought of this long ago with the first disobedience. Adam stood justifying himself, and then Eve tried it too. It didn't work then, and it won't ever work. God is not a liar. If He says something, you can count on it coming through.

So how does a person get out of this situation of having done wrong realizing there is a payment due? Society makes us pay for our crimes. Even if we admit we have done wrong, we still have to pay for the crime done.

What if someone paid the penalty for us? At first thought we assume all will say a loud yes, but in looking closer we see people who say they don't need anyone to pay for them or maybe don't feel deserving. This too is a lie. We all need to pay, and therefore, since we are lacking what is required, we need a savior, someone capable of forgiving our penalty.

The requirement is the death penalty. That was established from the beginning of time. You may not agree, just as you may not agree with some of man's laws. It doesn't matter whether you knew the law or not—you are still guilty if you break the law. Think of speeding and the consequences. You won't get out of the penalty by just saying you didn't know the speed limit.

Now if you're a Christian reading this, you are probably zipping through this like it is old news. However, since Jesus did die on the cross for us, we ought to do everything we can to show our gratitude. We can't justify ourselves when we do wrong by saying, "Well, I am just human" because we are no longer "just human."

You have the power of the living God in you. It should become much easier to turn away from sin. You have the vehicle that Christ paid for to take the great message *and* example to all who are hurting. If all of us could show Christ's example of love and forgiveness, the world wouldn't scream hypocrite in our faces.

I know we have not yet been made physically perfect and that there is the potential to fail, but why focus on those things that don't please the Lord? Jump whole-heartedly into reading the Bible and pouring out love to all you meet. It becomes fun too. Love can be contagious. Go out with the intention of infecting someone. Let forgiveness be contagious!

It is amazing to see how man lives by God's laws on his own terms, picking and choosing what he likes and dislikes. But God will not allow this to go unpunished. He is slow, not as men see it to let sin pass, but He is merciful, not wanting anyone to have to pay.

In the beginning He put animals to death for man's sake because death was the payment. It wasn't the perfect payment, but it was used as a down payment until the time it could be paid in full.

It makes perfect sense then to have a perfect payment from Jesus, who never broke the law. There has never been another perfect one. Believe it or not, that is your choice. But consider the consequences in choosing to pay it yourself. You have no payment of your own, absolutely none.

Christians must look at *trying to do things their way* as

taking it out of God's hands. Since God didn't give unforgiveness to you to use against others, how did you get it? It has to have been stolen! Well, that's a thought I am sure no one wants to have. I am not big enough to fight God for something. Besides, it is something for Him to handle. "Dearly beloved, avenge not yourselves, but rather give place unto wrath: for it is written, Vengeance is mine; I will repay, saith the LORD" (Romans 12:19).

Once again you are faced with the choice of life and death. Only you can choose. You will stand alone before God. What will be your justification for holding on to unforgiveness?

An inheritance is given to a person upon the death of another. It is the living person's responsibility to take what was given. If he chooses not to, then he gets nothing, no matter how much is waiting. So it is with the gift of forgiveness and justification. With Jesus' payment you are justified to stand before a holy and just God with full pardon for your crimes. No payment, no forgiveness; then you will receive what the law has designated. You choose. My opinion is that holding a grudge isn't worth going to hell for, no matter how huge the wrong that was done.

Again as Christians we have the privilege to approach a loving, forgiving God without fear of attack. However, if we hold on to grudges, we risk living this life with great disappointment and embarrassment, because in doing so we are withholding the love God has given us to share with others.

Now if you have taken the payment for sin from Jesus, there is a mandate with it. Since we are then justified only by accepting Jesus' payment, we are called to live as Jesus did in forgiving and loving others. We have ample provisions given to us to share with others. So life truly begins when we accept Jesus and the truth.

Life is about loving and forgiving, living with full gratitude to God for the payment. *An attitude of gratitude will be a place of grace.* Forgiveness then becomes the norm instead of the exception because we are able to live by His example.

To not have that payment leaves us empty and striving to come up with it on our own. Thus we experience disappointment, frustration, and bitterness toward others and ourselves. Jesus shouldn't be left in the closest for certain occasions. He is to go with us everywhere to achieve all He wants us to achieve through us.

If I hadn't found Jesus and received the payment for my crimes, I would have seen no point in forgiving anyone else, especially the ones who took part in my conception. I would want payment from them, not knowing they are incapable of making that payment.

Not only is Jesus payment for my crimes, but He is also payment for the crime someone else commits against me. He stands between me and my offender and says, "I have this covered. I made the payment on this too." It will have to be the offender to take the payment from Jesus now. So I can back off, say, "Thank you, Jesus," and go on with the plan He has for my life without the distractions of an offender.

Once God has forgiven us and there is mutual acceptance, we need not fear God. We may still suffer some of the consequences for bad choices, but condemnation is not there for the follower. Jesus justified us with his payment, thus giving us forgiveness. This is God's adoption process and the way we become His children. We can approach God knowing He accepts this payment in full. We are justified in truth and forgiven through Christ. He then welcomes us into His family.

BENEFITS OF FORGIVENESS

Well, if you choose to forgive others and receive forgiveness for yourself, there are many benefits. Not only will your spirit be set free, but you will also live healthier. The body has been shown to respond to thoughts of unforgiveness the same way it does to stress.

If you are still harboring bad feelings toward someone, notice how your body reacts as you speak the offender's name. The heart races and muscles tighten. What you can't see is the blood flow to your joints decreasing. Less blood flow makes it difficult for the body to remove wastes and reduces nutrients to the body. Digestion slows down and suffers.

Unforgiveness causes disease. The immune system is weakened, making it easier for disease, such as cancer, to attack the body. You might be aware that you are clenching your jaws. This promotes problems with joints and teeth. Headaches become more frequent.

If you're concentrating on unforgiveness for your offender, you are more likely to have accidents from not paying attention to your surroundings. Your mind is preoccupied with something other than life. Ever drive angry and not remember how you got to your destination?

Relationships with other people will suffer. Irritability and shortness of temper will spill over to family, friends, and co-workers. Bitterness affects all aspects of our lives.

It blocks the flow of God's love, and we all know what a wonderful feeling love is.

I was speaking to a woman who lived with unforgiveness for her cousin. She was overwhelmed with bitterness. She began seeing her health deteriorate and finally came to the realization that she was destroying her own body because she wouldn't let it go.

Remember the snake example? Doctors couldn't find a cure for this woman's ailments. Once she forgave and let go, healing began not only in her mind and soul but also in her body. *Many are sick and dying because they are holding onto the snake of bitterness and unforgiveness.*

The benefits of forgiveness are found in three dimensions: the mind, the spirit, and the body.

For your mind, forgiveness offers peace that passes all understanding. Once we have received forgiveness for our wrongs and have passed forgiveness on to our offenders, we are given a great reward of peace.

Sleep comes easy for those who rest in forgiveness. A gentle comfort knowing we are in right standing with the Lord is sweeter than the greatest earthly gain. Many people find it hard to sleep at night. Perhaps an evaluation of bitterness and unforgiveness is needed. People see a great difference once free of bitterness. Daily evaluation may be necessary, as the voices will want to come back and convince us not to forgive.

The peace that comes with forgiveness takes tension away from our body once the mind has made the choice to put away all that it is holding. Here is an exercise to prove this point. Hold on to something tightly for fifteen minutes. Release it and feel the weakness in your muscle. Holding on so tightly weakens us. We need to relax in our decision to forgive.

Our spirit is free to rest in the care of God himself when we allow him to take the unforgiveness from us. We must make a conscious declaration to Him that we will forgive and *act* in that forgiveness. We must choose with our mind, along with our mouth, and then our actions should follow. Feelings will be a bit slower, but if we continue in obedience to God's moral law, the feelings will come.

We can have full confidence that we are forgiven and there is no need to worry. God is not a liar.

The best benefit to forgiveness is eternity through God's forgiveness of our sins. We must then pass that forgiveness to others. I repeat this often for a purpose. It is crucial that this is grasped. God even says that if we don't forgive, we won't be forgiven. That is extremely important to say the least. It is a very good reason to choose His forgiveness and to give it away also.

Don't forget we must forgive ourselves. Forgiveness is worthless unless we forgive ourselves too. *Unforgiveness for ourselves will affect us as deeply as unforgiveness toward others.*

Our spirit is also free now to communicate with God. The barrier of unforgiveness and imperfection has been removed by Jesus' payment of death on the cross. We can hear God's Spirit speaking to ours, leading us to do what is right. This too is a daily recognition. To simply acknowledge this once will not give us continual power to succeed. A daily decision to do as Jesus did and to forgive continually is vital to success. You must live in the truth.

SIGNS OF GOD

People don't want to forgive sometimes because they are not fully aware there is a God. But He is the one who requires us to forgive if we wish to be forgiven. So this chapter is dedicated to signs of God's intervention. When we are aware of God in our lives, it gives us reason to believe Him. Believing makes it possible to follow His ways. Some people believe in Him only to blame God for the bad things that happen but don't see God working greatly for their good.

Yes, there are signs of God all around. Many see things that others can't even imagine. Maybe *that* is exactly why they can't see. We are open to being formed from goop or from apes, but the truth that God formed us is hard to accept because we have an enemy standing between us and God. We are the only ones who can step aside to see God. We may hear that small voice leading us in a direction or have a thought to do something we don't understand. Maybe it is God!

My dad died September 24, 2007. I had just spent three weeks in South Africa sharing my story and songs. I was on my flight back when my dad literally dropped dead. He had been healthy so this was totally unexpected. My husband didn't tell me until I was in the parking garage at my hometown airport. Richard didn't tell me anything, just avoided why my dad wasn't answering the phone. He said the phone was having problems. So when I arrived and was told my dad had died hours earlier, I went insane. How could this have happened when I was in South Africa for God's sake, literally? I knew it had been God because everything fell into place without me asking. People I didn't even know rallied to voluntarily make appointments for me to speak and sing. I felt like I was whisked away. My dad was proud of me. The last thing I said to my dad face to face as I was walking out the door was, "Now don't you go and die on me, ya hear!" He just smiled. We talked often of how I loved him and didn't want him to die any time soon. He always said he was ready to go and didn't want to live one hundred years. I came home to find he had indeed died.

I was so hurt and angry that God would do this. All I had asked was for Him to keep my dad safe until I returned. I pounded the dashboard of the van screaming, "Why? Why? Why?" Then I demanded my husband take me to the funeral home where my dad was.

I threw off my shoes wanting no hindrances to getting in there as quickly as possible. I was asked to wait for a few moments, and my mind raced everywhere but to an answer. I hadn't slept for about twenty-seven hours, and I was exhausted from the trip. *This must be a nightmare, and I will wake up shortly,* I told myself.

Then I heard the man say, "You can see him now."

There he was, lifeless, no big smile waiting. I prayed over my dad angrily that he come back to life. I know God was quite patient with me. How demanding I was, how totally like a child having a tantrum. I had just spent three weeks singing and speaking about how faithful God is, and this is how I chose to act in this opportunity. I was out of control. I was able, however, to maintain control outwardly for the sake of others. But the questions never left my mind, getting louder and louder.

Once my father was buried, I was left alone with my questions. All of a sudden I saw a flash as if I were having my picture taken. I was having a vision. I knew I was sitting in Job's chair. My heart began to race, and I knew I had done wrong. I began crying and saying, "I am sorry. I am sorry." Over and over again I said it.

God does speak to us. If we know His voice, we will hear Him. I heard a voice I *knew* was God say to me, "Who is this that darkens my counsel?" Job too had heard these words. God continued asking me all the questions He had asked Job, questions like, "Where were you when the foundations of the earth were formed?" and "Do you know where the snow is stored?" The questions kept coming as I cried, "I am sorry." It was horrible. I knew I had spoken without knowledge. I asked God fearfully why I had to hurt so much with my dad's dying. He said, "I want you to feel just a tiny bit of what I felt when I lost my son because of you."

Many people would say that wasn't God. He would never talk that way. Well, if I pushed my sweet daddy on earth too far, he would. So here is God who loves me more than my own father, so why not talk to me like the disrespectful child I was? Oh, it did hurt. But my eyes were opened to see that God was including me in an intimacy with Him. He wanted me to stop complaining and to be grateful.

I was very angry with God and felt justified. Deception clouded my thinking. (This is where some people harbor unforgiveness toward God.) The truth is that God has done nothing needing forgiveness! Then God showed me exactly what had happened during this time. He listed the truth of the situation, which was so different from my view. God said,

> He had spared me from watching my dad die. The
> three weeks I was away gave time for my husband
> and my dad to talk without me around.
> My dad was ready to go.
> My dad did not suffer at all and just dropped dead.

This was completely different from my selfish desires to hold on to my dad.

Some say God was quite harsh, but I see it as very loving way to take me and straighten out my thinking. I was miserable living in the lie. But once He showed me the truth, I was free to live again. We don't always like hearing the truth, but once we accept, it is nourishment to the soul. Our constant thought should be that God *is* real, that He knows what's best for us, and that His ways are the *only way* to freedom. We can't hold bitterness toward God. We don't understand His ways. And we certainly can never be justified before a holy and just God. When we realize we cannot be justified, we will seek to be forgiven instead. Forgiveness through the death of Jesus Christ is the greatest sign of God with us.

My trip to South Africa was not without signs of God too. I stayed at a beautiful bed and breakfast. Despite how tranquil and beautiful the surrounding, the owners were having difficulties with finances. They didn't have enough guests to pay the bills. I was the only one staying there at the time. The owner came to me asking me to pray for her. I did, and God revealed an unequal partner. So we asked God to make a way out. Then in a meeting with the owners, both husband and wife (without the partner), God told me to ask about their tithing. The answer the husband gave was, "We give what we can." That was the incorrect answer. God says to give at least ten percent of our income. Sometimes we think we don't have enough, so we cut God out first and pay him whatever, if anything, that we have when we're done. I have found over and over again that if I do that, I will always have less than if I give to God first. He gives us a promise in

> "You are under a curse—the whole nation of you—because you are robbing me. Bring the whole tithe into the storehouse, that there may be food in my house. Test me in this," says the LORD Almighty, "and see if I will not throw open the floodgates of heaven and pour out so much blessing that you will not have room enough for it."
>
> Malachi 3:9

So I read this to the couple. Immediately the man said that he would do this. That very next day, every room was occupied. They couldn't explain how that happened except that God honored the intentions of the couple. We were ecstatic, but the miracle to follow was more than incredible. Days later this couple had their own family reunion. God told the woman (owner) to talk to a particular male cousin, whom she hadn't known very well, about her business and the struggles to pay bills. The man asked for a time to pray in one of the rooms and went away. In about five minutes the man returned and said he would purchase the place for $1.3 million. The couple was shocked. Happy, but also disappointed to lose their place, they agreed to sell it. To their amazement, the new owner turned around and just *gave* them the deed back! They were given $1.3 million days after their commitment to tithe.

Yes, God is most faithful. We can trust Him to do great things!

Years ago I agreed to go with a friend to Uganda. But in the months prior, thoughts filled my mind about spiders there. I was filled with so much fear that I cancelled my trip. It would be years later when God would reveal an important lesson to me.

It was the first night in my new home on April 15, 2003. Our bed hadn't been delivered, so we slept on the mattress on the floor. During the night I was bitten by a brown recluse spider. I had actually been bitten twice since my cancellation of the trip to Uganda, but I thought nothing of it. With immediate antibiotics, it was no problem at all. But this time I postponed going to the doctor, thinking I would just take care of it on my regular appointment four days later. By the time that day came, the infection had spread and the area was black. Even with antibiotics, the infection spread and poisoned my system. I was literally delirious. Hospitalized and requiring surgery gave me time to think. Actually, one day in the hospital I heard (in my mind) God's voice asking me what I was doing. That sounded rather strange because God knows all. So I replied in my thoughts back to Him, "You know, Lord, I am in here because of a spider bite." But he asked again, "Why are you here?" As I was answering again, "Because of a spi…" I stopped. I knew what this was about now. God then told me, "You can go anywhere in the world where you think you are safe without me, and you won't be safe. But if you go with me anywhere in the world, you are safe." It had taken three times for me to get the message. I certainly get it now. I will go wherever God sends me without fear.

Another very impacting time with the Lord actually started out very disappointing. Have you ever prayed and just felt like it was useless? Have you felt you're talking to the ceiling and nothing is happening? You are not alone.

I recall one day when I really needed God to do something. I just wanted to know He was there. Nothing happened. No feelings, no great move of God—nothing came. I became very upset and angry. I stood up and yelled, "Where are you? Can you hear me?" I wasn't reverent at all. Extremely frustrated and determined to get God's attention, I began thinking. I remembered someone saying that God inhabits the praises of His people. Well, I knew I was one of His people, so I told Him I would just praise Him until He showed up. With a bad attitude I began listing the great things of God. "You're the creator of the universe. You made us in your image. You sacrificed your life for me."

With each praise and declaration, my spirit and temperament changed. I was different because I was focusing on who *He* is and not what I wanted from Him. All of a sudden the presence of God was so strong I was brought to my knees. I was ashamed of my attitude and asked for forgiveness. Arrogance had turned to great humility, and there is where I felt the embrace of the Almighty God.

It is not in our demands that God meets our needs, but it is in our submission and acknowledgment of who He is that we find provision. If you find your prayers are going nowhere, try praising and dwelling on whom God is and what He has already done for us.

I saw angels once when I was praying at a friend's house. First, I saw demonic looking eyes strangely looking at me through posters on the wall of a friend's daughter's room. She hadn't told me the daughter was into some strange things. When I told her I thought there were demons in her daughter's room, she said she knew that. She wanted to know if I was aware of them. We went in and started praying for them to go. Just at that moment I saw two angels in white standing on each side of the window. The stranger thing about this was seeing them outside and through the ceiling. They were huge, maybe twenty feet tall. One was blond with curly hair, and the other had a dark complexion with dark hair.

In less time than it takes to read this, it all happened. Gray smoke of some sort was sucked out from the posters, flying right between the two angels, and immediately they were gone. It was like the demons were sucked out by a vacuum!

I saw angels another time when I was praying in a church. I happened to look up for some reason while we were all holding hands and praying. We were the team of singers about to practice for Sunday service. When I looked up and around, I saw so many angelic figures hovering over us and the church. It was a magnificent sight.

At one Passover celebration I went to a few years ago, a wonderful site appeared. As the dancers were dancing, I saw a mist or cloud of some sort going in and out of the dancers. It looked as if a spirit was actually dancing with them, although it had no definitive form.

I felt the presence of the Lord so strong that I could

hardly stand it. Later I learned that the prayer of the dancers was to have the Lord dance with them. My eyes were open to see. We must be open to know, trust, and see what God is doing.

These examples are so miniscule compared to the things some people see. I write these things to say that I believe in the spirit world. If you've lived long enough, there will be something you won't be able to explain. There are signs of God all around. Start looking for them. Demons are real too. They are determined beings with one goal. Their goal is to keep you from ever knowing the love of God. But God is there to overcome every time.

A story that a friend told me is nothing short of incredible. She was living in New York with her two-year-old. She wasn't a Christian and in fact was disgusted with the Christian at the laundromat who continually told her about Jesus. She even spit on him and cursed him.

One night Nina came home to find a man was there waiting for her in her apartment. She didn't notice him at first and put her young son to bed. But when she went to her own bedroom, he jumped on her. He had a stocking to cover his face. She was beaten, raped, and left for dead, but she awoke and tried to get up. The man was still there and came at her with a sheet to strangle her. Nina remembered the man at the laundromat and said "Jesus, if you're real, help me."

Just at that moment, she saw a greenish bright light come from the window and hit her attacker right between the eyes, and he fled. She then ran with her son to the neighbors' for help. It was discovered that this man was a serial rapist and killer. She was able to help police capture and identify him. He was convicted and put away.

The police were amazed at her escape. Others had not escaped.

Nina is a walking display of God's protection and love. Nina's life has been one episode after another of God's hand reaching into her life.

If we search, we will find God. If we step out in faith as small as a mustard seed, as was evident with Nina, we will see the hand of God.

They instigate bitterness and unforgiveness to keep you from seeing signs of God. You know that when you're angry and bitter, you don't notice many things around you. If you can overlook things when you're angry that are visible to all in the natural, how much easier will it be to overlook the spiritual when you are angry?

I don't know anyone (not even atheists) that *don't* want a sign that God is real. But few are willing to do what is necessary to see. If you live in unforgiveness evil has won and you will never experience the fullness of God or see His hand at work.

Well, God is definitely around. We can see evidence everywhere. It is just logical that there is a designer, but there are things unexplainable. Some doctors are now incorporating prayer in the healing process. In fact, I know one doctor that says he has brought healing to more people by the power of God than when he was operating as a neurosurgeon. He has witnessed the power God gives us through our thoughts. Miracles in no other words have been seen. No hoaxes, no magic. Relying on God is the key.

I have personally had healing in my own body. Once I had great chest pains that got me a ride in the ambu-lance to the nearest hospital. They discovered a black spot on my lung and insisted I see a doctor immediately. That doctor told me he had no answers but that it could be malignant. We'd have to wait three months to see if something developed.

Something came out of my mouth that my ears were even surprised to hear. I told the doctor that in three months I'd come back and have no spot anywhere because Jesus would heal me. He admitted that something did happen sometimes that he couldn't explain. He wished me the best, and I left.

I knew God had done something. Three months later I had the tests done again, and just like I had said, there were no spots, not even one. Jesus had healed me.

Still another time I had a lump in my breast. I went for prayer at my church on a Wednesday evening, and while we were praying I felt a warm sensation in my breast. I knew I was healed. That Friday when I went for sonograms and mammograms, they looked at the results and asked me why I was there. I told them the whole story, and they stared in amazement.

Healing *does* happen. I know that God does it for us.

I know we can't put God in a box but also that He is not a liar. We can take Him at His word. When we know His voice, we can step out in faith and do what He asks us to. It will never hurt another person. It may cause them to become angry, but we will always be looking after the best interest of others and not ourselves. We will see wonderful things if we just trust Him.

Can I answer the questions of why and why not? No, but I know that if God truly loves me, He will take care of me, seeing to it that nothing will destroy me—my spirit. The body is a temporary thing, but my spirit will live for eternity. I want to do all that is going to be best for my spirit even if it conflicts with what my body wants. So I live with the belief that truly the "what ifs" are possible with God.

What if God speaks to us? God does speak to us in many ways. Here is an example of Him speaking to me in daily life.

I love cats and have had them for many years, even growing up with them. They all have a different personality. So God showed me how people are through observation of my cats. If you pay attention, you will see God's hand in your life. He will show you things that you never thought about.

One cat was the epitome of "scaredy-cat." If I wore a windbreaker and swished my arms, Freckles would nearly jump to the ceiling in fear. He was always looking around and cowering. This was shown to me to be people, believers and nonbelievers alike, controlled by fear, unable to concentrate on anything else.

Then there was Smokey. At the animal shelter she was all show, loving on us, purring, saying, "I'm gonna make you love me." And we fell for it. She was beautiful. We got her home, and a whole different attitude came out, more like, "Hey, thanks for the ride. Now leave me alone!" She wasn't affectionate any longer. This is the person that starts out at church needing the Savior but once forgiven says, "Thanks for the ride" and wants to be left alone. They will do whatever they want just because they were "saved" and don't want to be told anything.

Next there's Sassy, Freckles' sister. Sassy was always there when I was feeling badly. She seemed to have a radar that just knew I needed some love. She slept with me and was always by my side. She walked with me and even "talked" with me.

But then we rescued a cat from the pound called Oreo. Oreo was living at my friend's apartment and when she moved was picked up by the city pound. My friend called me crying to help her and Oreo. So she paid for the adoption, and Oreo came home with me.

Now, Sassy wasn't happy about this at all. Like the older son in the prodigal's story, she was offended that I would take in this cat. She went off and slept in the library, not really wanting to socialize with me anymore. She let her offense ruin our relationship. Like people who are offended, she held a grudge and became sick. She died with cancer.

Oreo has never left my side. He is so grateful and totally understands he was rescued and saved. Once friendly with the world and everyone that walked up to him, he now runs to my bedroom when people come over. He first makes sure they are safe after I have talked with them for a while, and then he comes out.

This reminds me of Christians. We were once doing everything everyone else did and feeling free to roam the streets. Once Christ has saved us, we know that all is not safe, and we should allow God to first check things out for us. We are safe only where He is.

Lastly, there is Dusty. Dusty is a beautiful, blue-eyed, champagne colored cat. He knows he's gorgeous. He used to cause grief to Sassy just because he was bored. He would bully her. She was older, but that didn't matter to him. He would strut around, never knowing a bad day in his life. We had him from the time he was a kitten. Stuck up and unappreciative, he would give us attention on his terms.

However, when my dad moved in with us, something changed. My dad stayed home all the time. Dusty would come around to get his head rubbed, and my dad obliged him. After a while Dusty became Daddy's best buddy. We even called him Daddy's "dog." Daddy whistled and Dusty came running.

This is an illustration of people who seem to be untouchable. They just need someone to really stick it out with them and show them love by spending time with them. Love can penetrate hearts. Even animals respond with consistency. We shouldn't give up so quickly. So what if God can use our surroundings to teach us? What if we keep our ears and eyes open to see God? The more we believe in what ifs, the more open we are to forgiveness.

I don't know if you played "pretend" when you were a kid, but my younger brother and I did. He'd say, "What if you be the police, and I be the bad guy?" or "What if you be the horse, and I be the cowboy?" (I grew up on a farm with no Indians, just cowboys and horses.) We could always save the day. We were the heroes in our own stories.

But there came a day when our excited "what ifs" became frightened "what ifs." I can't even remember when it happened. Maybe it was the first time someone laughed at our "what ifs." Maybe there was a bit of a struggle to keep them alive, but we became weak without support. Then our dreams, hopes, and joyful "what ifs" died, and so did our ability to see God at work. Fear keeps us from seeing, and fear keeps us from forgiving. They were replaced with "What if I fail?" "What if they laugh at me again?" "What if I get hurt?" and a multitude of other fear provoked "what ifs." Our childlike thoughts were replaced with what we thought was mature and logical. But have we forgotten one of the best tools God has given us. "What if" is really the beginning of faith and the door to seeing signs of God. Will it grow or will it die?

The young usually possess more positive "what ifs" because they have less history of failure. Ever notice how children can fight and then get over it? It is usually the parents holding on to unforgiveness! Children will say, "What if I lose my friend?" while parents say, "What if it happens again and my child gets hurt?" We aren't teaching forgiveness, but instead we are reinforcing unforgiveness.

What if you were able to get your wonderful, adventurous "what ifs" back? What if I could show you that "what ifs" were meant to be carried with you all your life?

Successful people hold on to the positive "what ifs" no matter what, while others cling to the destructive "what ifs." Ever tell a person your idea or dream, and immediately they're saying, "What if it doesn't work, or what if something bad happens?" What if you turned it back on them with, "What if it does work?" You could also say, "Well, I won't know until I try."

You can't give up so easily. My mom used to say, "Anything worth having is worth fighting for." I don't think she meant that literally at the time, but sometimes things do require a battle, whether physically or just mentally and spiritually. Life is a battle no matter how you look at it. There's always some sort of struggle. Forgiving people is one of those struggles. But there can always be the wonderful "what ifs."

What if we were able to stop the negative voices that we even tell ourselves? You know the things you say: "I was so stupid. I never can do anything right. I hate myself for that. Things will never change." The same song and dance humans have played for all of history. But the ones that succeeded are the ones that never gave up. They fell but told themselves, "What if I get up and do it again? I might succeed this time." Forgiving yourself will help you to see positive "what ifs."

We are what we believe and what we think on every moment. A perfect example is the time I found out I was conceived in rape. One moment I was ready to die because of my thinking, and then hours later I chose to believe, "What if Jesus did love me enough to give his life for me?" Then I had a responsibility to him to follow through. A woman, without having a clue what was going on, said to me, "I don't know what is going on with you, but God knew you before you were ever conceived!" I chose to say, "I believe it!" At that very moment, my "what if" changed to a "what if" of wonderful proportions. What if God loved me so much that he told this woman to say exactly the words I needed to hear? What if God was responsible for my existence?

What if He has a great and specific plan for my life—for your life? Now life in a literal instant *can* change. I was asked a great question. "Who were you before you were told about your conception?" Hmmm. I had great faith, and I knew I was loved by God Almighty. But so quickly "what ifs" enter our minds ready to destroy. It is a choice to re-install the positive "what ifs."

When I found my birthmother and was told eight men had raped her, negative thoughts rushed in again. I began crying, but my mom said, "Stop crying. I've forgiven those men and look what God has done. He has brought you back to me!" Wow! My "What if there was hope?" back years ago came to be true.

Wonderful "what ifs" are possible if we don't give up. Most of our life is a choice. In America we are given so many choices that we become confused. Instead of thinking, *What if I don't do the right thing?* think, *What if I can do the right thing with the help of the Holy Spirit?*

In all that we do as Christians, we must go back to the Word of God for our standard. What if we only did what Jesus really would do? What if we believed his word as truth?

There are so many "what ifs" for us to explore in our journey here on earth. What good is it to always do the bad "what if"? So you fail; what if you keep going, knowing the Bible says that "and we know that in all things God works for the good of those who love him, who have been called according to his purpose" (Romans 8:28).

> Finally, brothers, whatever is true, whatever is noble, whatever is right, whatever is pure, whatever is lovely, whatever is admirable—if anything is excellent or praiseworthy—think about such things.
>
> Philippians 4:8

What if?

> "I tell you the truth, anyone who has faith in me *(What if)* will do what I have been doing. He will do even greater things than these, because I am going to the Father."
>
> John 14:12

Everything that does not come from faith is sin. What if we do everything in faith?

Romans 14:23

Examine yourselves to see whether you are in the faith; test yourselves. (*What if*) Do you not realize that Christ Jesus is in you—unless, of course, you fail the test? What if you do pass the test and you realize you can do all things through him who strengthens you?

11 Corinthians 13:5

So those who have faith are blessed along with Abraham, the man of faith. What if you believe you will be blessed?

Galatians 3:9

Therefore, prepare your minds for action; be self-controlled; set your hope (*what ifs*) fully on the grace to be given you when Jesus Christ is revealed.

1 Peter 1:13

What if we could do this:

When we are cursed, we bless; when we are persecuted, we endure it.

1 Corinthians 4:12

We *can* live with great "what ifs" such as What if this year is the best my marriage has ever been? What if I choose to love those who are mean to me? What if I hear the voice of God and respond quickly? What if we can be conquerors, hey, *more* than conquerors?" or even "What if I could be like those timeless fairytale dreams of being royalty, the child of a king?"

Well, the truth is we can. With Jesus we have an adoption into royalty. It's time to realize our position. How great is the love the Father has lavished on us, that we should be called *"children of God"* (1 John 3:1). "What ifs" are a tool given by God, and if we use them his way, we will be able to accomplish great things. Believe and use them with the guidance of the Holy Spirit that has been promised you and see your "what ifs" turn to reality. What if we stand before God one day, and he says to us, "Well done, good and faith *full* servant!"

TURNING HURTS INTO BLESSINGS

Now that you know forgiveness is the beginning of life, you are able to take every situation and turn it around for your victory. God wants to bless you and actually is watching and waiting to disburse those blessings to you. If you do not follow through with actions after you say you forgive, your blessings will be blocked. Your blessings will be held back until you proceed.

His hand will be evident when we are doing what He has instructed. Sin, bitterness, and unforgiveness block our view of God. Whether we agree to submit or not, God is still God and will call us to account one day. It is better to turn your hurts into blessings by giving your hurts *and* yourself to God. Many people feel that they have to give up so much. We will only lose the bad and gain all the good He has for us when we turn to Him completely.

The sign that you have your blessings flowing is your peace. I have heard of people trying to justify doing wrong and saying they have a peace about it. If it goes against God's moral law and His heart, you have been given a false peace by the evil one.

Here's an important point. I can't forgive one moment then pick it up again where I left off. There is no healing in that. There are no blessings there either. If I choose to walk in forgiveness, I will possibly see greater blessings in relationships than before the offense. My former mother-in-law is a perfect example of loving through the offense. I wasn't a Christian when I divorced her son. I had married him at eighteen. I loved his mother as my own. I hurt my ex-husband deeply, and it would be years before he would hear me ask his forgiveness. His mother loved me dearly, and I can't imagine how deep her pain was, which I caused. For years she prayed, and whenever I talked with her, she was always loving. It brings me to tears thinking about her faithfulness to God and to me. She only showed Jesus. She will reap rewards in heaven, but here she is cherished by all. I would die for this woman, and I consider her a mother to me. She never gave up on me. She even calls me her daughter, and I call her mom. I didn't reunite with her son. Many years later I married my current husband. For nineteen years she has accepted him and loved him also. What an example of God's love for us! While we were still sinners, He loved us. And she loved me that way too. Hers is a life remembered and cherished for generations. At this writing she is eighty-six, pure and loving as always. She is healthy and full of joy. She *is* living the power of love. I believe it is because love ruled in her mind and body. She chose to follow Jesus even when it hurt. She chose to turn the hurts into blessings through forgiveness. She could have ended our relationship and held on to unforgiveness. Because she forgave me, I now will do anything for her. That is her blessing. We too can turn an offender into a blessing by forgiving.

Consider what happened to my birthmother. The pain she felt was beyond words. She could have wasted away with bitterness. Instead she believed God was faithful. She never gave up. She has joy unspeakable with no regrets for doing what was right. Today she and I have a great relationship. Had she chosen abortion, she would not be a hero. She is my hero, and I make it known to her as well as everyone else. She turned her hurts into a blessing for herself, me, and my adopted parents.

Suppose a person has hurt you and does not want reconciliation because they think you have hurt them too. Maybe you want to grow forward, but they do not. While you cannot force someone to bless you in return, you can know that God will continue to bless you if you act right. You must trust him fully. God is not a liar. He has told us that what we sow is what we will reap. We can expect it *will* happen even if it is slow in coming. Eternity is real.

You must have an attitude that is pleasing to Him. I must say it does hurt, and I have personally heard "I don't want to be your friend" from a family member. Wow, that cut through my heart. I want to be friends with everyone but most certainly with a loved one. Family is so important to me. What should my response be? The same as Jesus said when He was being killed on the cross. "Father forgive them for they do not know what they are doing" (Luke 23:24).

I must admit I didn't respond in a loving manner, but I reacted out of hurt. Maybe my excuse could have been that I was affected by the sleeping pill I had taken. It was after I had gone to bed and I was awakened. Being half asleep could be used to justify myself. Wrong! There is no justification. I was wrong for my part no matter what! I was, however, very quick to call that person the next morning and ask for forgiveness. My blessing was felt immediately by the peace I had, even though there was no reciprocation or acceptance. It may take years before I see the greater blessing. But I did turn the hurt around when I asked for forgiveness and gave forgiveness. (I was careful not to *give* that forgiveness out loud for fear of making things worse.)

Some may say that I shouldn't be the one to ask for forgiveness because I was the one hurt. *My* actions are all mine! I have the responsibility to continue to love and treat this person as I would want Jesus to treat me. No matter how hurt I may be, God requires and enables me to be loving. This is a true test for me, proving just how committed I am to Jesus. With Jesus there is great power, but the key is to submit fully to Him. He won't be Savior if He can't be *Lord!*

If I allow my flesh to take over, I will run away in rejection or retaliate in anger. No blessings there! But I recall even Jesus had people doubting and not wanting to be His friend. He continued to love. So if He in His perfection could be criticized and rejected, then I certainly can expect it in my humanness.

Blessings will overtake us if we walk with Jesus. I must guard my heart to make sure no ill feelings take over. Our greatest vulnerability to bitterness comes right after an offense. The sooner we take action against it, the easier it is to remove the seed of bitterness. Once that root has grown into a tree, it will take much more effort to remove it. *Pray for the person who has offended you and watch that wonderful peace flow.*

In the Bible there have been numerous situations that show blessings given for blessing an enemy. Haggai blessed his enemy with provisions, as they were his captives. He released them, and they never attacked him again. Just think if he had treated them badly or destroyed them. Their families would have sought revenge.

Also there was Joseph in the Bible, who was treated horribly by his brothers and sold into slavery. A famine came, and these same brothers were in the presence of Joseph, the brother they sold. He was ruling under the Pharaoh. Not only did he *not* hold a grudge, he sent everyone away and revealed himself privately to these brothers who couldn't even recognize him. He said what they meant for evil God used for good, even their own good. He turned his hurts into blessing the offenders.

Never underestimate doing good.

Some people operate in only part of the truth. That is how Satan deceives and traps us. Sometimes God's principles are taken without crediting him. While there are positive results from using His principles, the full benefit is not gained without submitting fully to God. You can enjoy a ride in the car as long as it has gas; however, once the gas is gone, someone needs to refuel, or you're not going anywhere. God has an endless supply of "gas" or blessings. Without Him you will only reap the natural, earthly blessings available to everyone. To achieve the ability to turn hurts into blessings will require a full connection to the one who supplies all our needs—God alone.

The Bible says to be still *and* know He is God. Then the peace beyond understanding will come. Otherwise you get a false peace for a while that keeps you from knowing God. Remember the goal of the evil one is to keep us from knowing the love of God and His forgiveness. *We turn those hurts into blessings when we overcome the temptation to follow the flesh.*

Another way to turn hurts into blessings is to take the hurts we have felt and turn with compassion to those who have been hurt too. Misery loves company? Not exactly. We don't join them for an all out pity party, but instead we can supply them with what they have lost.

Have you lost a loved one? Turn to someone else and comfort them in their time of pain. Are you stressed about children? Offer to take care of someone else's to give them a break. (You'll appreciate your own time more afterwards.) Did you get pregnant out of wedlock? Don't spend time condemning yourself. Ask for forgiveness and let God use you to help others avoid the mistake. Do look at your problem long enough to recognize it in others. Take what God says about you and the problem. Believe Him to set yourself free and to offer freedom to others. Ask missionaries why they risk hardship, even death, to do what they do. They find that the blessings—the joy—far outweigh the sufferings. Get out there and stop looking inward. Look out and upward for your blessing. Unless Jesus lives inside you, there is no hope in finding solutions within yourself. That's another half-truth—"All you need is inside you." Only if Jesus is Lord over your heart will it satisfy forever.

IF THEY CAN DO IT, SO CAN YOU

So you're probably reading this book for a couple of reasons. Maybe you were curious, or maybe you needed inspiration to get through something of your own. Well, this chapter is devoted to stories of people who went from victim/offended to victor/healed. Hopefully these stories will get you on the way to your own forgiveness.

> For it is commendable if a man bears up under the pain of unjust suffering because he is conscious of God. But how is it to your credit if you receive a beating for doing wrong and endure it? But if you suffer for doing good and you endure it, this is commendable before God.
>
> 1 Peter 2:19–20

God doesn't want us to endure for the sake of endurance. I will say if you are in a sexually or physically abusive situation, please seek help. Forgiveness doesn't mean allowing people to continue the abuse. There is no glory in self martyrdom.

Viktor Frankl survived the Nazi death camp at Auschwitz. He really proved that circumstances do have the power to keep you imprisoned in your mind. He demonstrated ultimate freedom as the ability "to choose one's attitude in any given set of circumstances, to choose one's own way." Our mind is one, if not *the* most powerful tool given to us by God. Our minds create and destroy. Should we not choose to think thoughts that create power to live free?

Gwen Spinks is a vibrant, determined woman focused on God. Helping others is her passion. She has adopted children, created homes for the homeless, and loved on everyone she meets. But looking at her past finds a most horrific offense.

She was a sweet little girl with all the dreams a little girl could have. At ten Gwen's mother dressed her in a pretty dress. Her mother then asked her if she wanted a "job." Gwen was excited about earning money, thinking she would wash dishes for the neighbor or maybe rake leaves. The worst imaginable thing happened. Gwen's own mother prostituted her out to old men. How could a mother do this to her own child? This went on for years, and Gwen's mother would tell her she would have to continue if she wanted to have the things they had.

We are outraged at such a thing, and we ourselves want to hold a grudge against such a person. But the unimaginable happened. Gwen found Jesus and did a very unnatural thing. She forgave her mother and those men! It is not magic. It was a decision to follow what Jesus taught. When I asked Gwen what she gained out of forgiving them, she said without hesitation, "Freedom, of course." All of us who have forgiven unnaturally can attest to the power in releasing it to God. Now Gwen is a powerful minister herself with her own book, *From Prostitution to the Pulpit and Preaching*. Gwen heads up an organization called Mega Harvest Ministries in Michigan. What a great example of turning evil around to inspire her and make a difference in our world.

A woman I met years ago also was hurt deeply by a parent. I'll call her May (not her real name). This young woman watched her mother die of cancer when she was only fourteen years old. If that wasn't traumatic enough, her father came to her and, while threatening to kill himself, forced himself on his innocent and pure daughter. She was a virgin. Again our blood boils to think of such selfishness. She was frightened and in such a horrible state of mind that it took her nine months to work up the courage to confide in an aunt. The aunt went to a minister who talked to the father. May had grown up in the church and never had any problems with her father before. But that was still no excuse for his actions. Once the minister talked to her father, he agreed to stop. However, there was another incident when he tried again. May refused to let it happen again and protested vehemently. The father never attempted to hurt her again. She could forgive, but she also learned to say no. Forgiveness isn't about allowing someone to physically hurt you. But she did treat him better than we know he deserved. May told me God had given her other areas to help her with affirmation. She was named city beauty queen and had many friends. There still remained a feeling of unworthiness upon getting married, though. She told her husband about what her father had done before they married, but it later turned out that he couldn't handle it. After having two children, he left May for another woman. May would years later console the same woman that took her husband. She continued to express her commitment to God through her forgiveness in most difficult situations.

Forgiveness and kindness was a must for May's survival. She had to stay focused. Some are thinking that this is foolish to have these things happen and not be angry with God. But May stayed faithful. When May was eighteen, her father had asked for forgiveness. Years later she would have to forgive him again. May's father had remarried, but even after many, many years, he had not confided in his wife about his crime against his daughter. Then one day May's father had a stroke, making him very conscious of his mortality. So he felt compelled to tell his wife what had happened. I suppose he wanted to make himself look better, so he lied to his wife and told her May was consenting. So May's stepmother attacked her verbally, and May once again had to live through it all. This time it was worse because now she was being accused of participating. The old saying "adding insult to injury" was evident here. May had previously had a good relationship with her stepmother, but after her father confessed, things changed. The stepmother crossed May's name off her will and continued to believe May had consented to sex with her father. Now May's stepmother is no longer living, and her father is not well. He lives in an assisted living home but requires much time and assistance from May. Because May is a Christian, walking out her faith, she takes care of her father. He has never tried to fix what he did by lying to his wife. Today after surviving breast cancer, May is now taking care of her own father, who has deeply wounded her. She had the choice to love her enemy and honor her father at the same time.

The thought of honoring a man like that is appalling. But God does not stipulate whether that father is to be honorable before we honor him. People can call her stupid or co-dependent, but she is *free*. Free from bitterness and self pity, she knows the intimate relationship of God that seems so bizarre to others.

Does God condone what May's father did? Of course He doesn't. There are no real answers to why things happen or are allowed to happen. But those who go through all these things and cling to God know what only few people know. It is no easy task, but there is power in God to forgive.

I met Noble Alexander many years ago when I was working with Voice of the Martyrs. His name was most fitting. He was a noble man indeed, with great integrity and unwavering faith, eyes so gentle you'd think he lived a life sitting on the beach. No one could imagine what this man had to endure. In his book, *I Will Die Free*[5], Noble talks about "one of the champions of love, Sergio Bravo, a young prisoner of slight build." This young man was in a Cuban prison as a Christian. Nobel Alexander says of this man, "He had made it his daily mission to spread the principle of love triumphing over hate to anyone who would listen. 'You can rise above your natural human passions in your service for Christ,' Sergio claimed, not a simple task while living in an environment of deprivation, wanton cruelty, and brutish torment.[6]" Noble knew personally the torture of that Cuban prison.

Today when an American does some insulting act to a prisoner, the whole world demands recourse. But while we are held to a higher standard because of our foundations in God, the world around us does as they please. People know right from wrong; they just choose not to do it. We find many people believing we should be kind to our enemies in a prison situation, but what about our day to day "enemies"? We can live with forgiveness for everyone if we choose to seek the power from God alone.

Christians choose to love and treat others as we want to be treated because that was a mandate of Jesus. He too was tortured and felt immeasurable pain, all the while asking God the father to forgive his offenders. So His actions are our example. This is how people are able to forgive horrendous crimes.

Noble spent twenty years as a political prisoner in Castro's Cuba, one of the most inhumane and brutal prison systems on earth. He was determined to stay alive and live by the standards of his God. His wife even divorced him, but he never gave up on God. Twenty four years later she asked for his forgiveness. He said he had forgiven her the day she divorced him.

Noble said, "I have no time for bitterness." He also said he would not allow himself "to be devoured by the cancer of hate." He said, "I rejoice. I sing. I laugh. I celebrate, because I know that my God reigns supreme over all the forces of evil and destruction Satan has ever devised. And best of all—my God reigns supreme in me!"

He was beaten unmercifully, fed maggot-infested waste, and forced to stay crouched down in a box the size of a coffin for months. He never lost his focus. Noble died several years ago, an inspiration to all who met him. I know he has no regrets.

Another man and woman, who are my personal inspiration to continue loving, were Richard and Sabina Wurmbrand. Richard lived in prison for fourteen years, three of which were spent in solitary confinement. His crime? He was a pastor and Christian.

Sabina too spent many years in prison being told her

husband was dead. Their son was hiding with friends when she was taken to prison for being a Christian in Romania. They were finally ransomed out and then brought to the U.S. united as a family again. When I spoke with this couple, the sweetest aroma of love came from them like I have never known. Gentleness in their eyes was the overflow of their hearts. Some people can say they forgive but still have the lingering effects of their pain. This couple knew true freedom in their forgiveness. Richard was beaten so badly on his feet that he could not walk, but he went everywhere spreading the love of Jesus. His wonderful book, *Tortured for Christ*, is a testament to something amazing.

Over and over again, I have talked to people who have been tortured for their faith and come away with the peace that passes all understanding. Both Richard and Sabina are with the Lord now and surely grateful that they stayed faithful to Him. They were free here on earth from the constraints and weight of unforgiveness. No one could force them to live with hatred. I had the chance to have some time alone with Sabina at a conference once. I had to ask her this question: "If there was one most important thing you could tell me that you have learned, what would it be?"

Without hesitation and with a smile that lit up the room, she said, "Love Jesus."

I just looked at her. I already knew that. My mind was trying to figure this out. This was too simple. Or was it? She repeated herself. It was as if she'd said new words because I got it. If I loved Jesus, really loved Jesus, all things would work out for my good and His. That is the power to overcome evil. However, it is always a choice.

Rosalyn Jennings of Phoenix, Arizona, had a rough start, but her uncle came to the rescue, raising her as his own. She loved her uncle just as a person loves a father. Then something happened, and she lost contact with him when she was an adult. She felt someone she knew was keeping her messages from him. Dwelling on thoughts of why, how, and how dare this person do that to her, she only became more bitter toward that person. That is exactly how bitterness works. You have to continue thinking about it to make it bigger and stronger. Time went on, and the feelings grew worse. So did Rosalyn's health. She went to several doctors, but no one could give her a diagnosis. They had no idea what was wrong with her. Her health continued to worsen when she realized she needed to forgive that person who came between her and her uncle. Once she did that, her health returned. She now has a program called *The Power of Forgiveness* on Internet radio, *blogtalk.com*. She has personally seen the physical effects that bitterness and unforgiveness have on one's health. It does matter. She now devotes her time to helping others live a healthy and free life through forgiveness. I was on the phone line when one young man called into Rosalyn's show. He had been attacked in his home by burglars only weeks earlier. He was talking about the miracle God gave him. Doctors said he should have been in recovery for months, and instead it was one week. But what I heard on this call was the miracle of his words. He said he couldn't let hate take over. This young man chose to forgive and move on with his life. I believe his healing was due to his forgiveness toward his attackers.

In New York, many hard things happen, but forgiving an attacker is harder if one tries to do so in the natural. We never know all the benefits of forgiveness.

James Robison, television host and founder of *Life Today*, knows the freedom of forgiveness too. This is his story in his own words.

"I was born in poverty, the result of a forced sexual relationship. An alcoholic forced himself on a practical nurse caring for his elderly father, and I was conceived. The result of that experience was ultimately my birth in the charity ward of St. Joseph Hospital in Houston, Texas.

"My mother, Myra Wattinger, placed an ad in a Houston newspaper after my birth asking for someone to care for her little boy. A pastor and his wife, Rev. and Mrs. H.D. Hale, responded to the ad. They took me into their home, and I stayed with them until I was five years old. I called them Mommy and Daddy.

"On numerous occasions, my mother would come and visit me and even take me away for short periods of time. It was always a difficult experience, but the Hales explained to me that this was my mother and they were my mommy and daddy. Although confused, I tried to accept this as the way it was. I would spend many lonely days and nights with people I didn't know while my mother ran errands and took care of other matters.

"Apparently, the short visits were not enough for my mother. When I was five years old, she came and took me away from my mommy and daddy. I can remember hiding under the bed and literally digging my fingernails into the wooden floor as she pulled me, kicking and screaming, from beneath the bed. I did not want to go, but I had no choice.

"We departed the greater Houston area and went to Austin, where for the next ten years I moved at least fifteen times from one very difficult situation to the next. My mother married a man who could neither read nor write and was in his mid-sixties at the time. To say we were poor almost seems an understatement."

James enjoyed getting presents for birthdays and Christmas from these wonderful people (the Hales). However, on his ninth birthday, it all stopped. He was devastated, not knowing that his mother was the one that had stopped the Hales and James' aunt from sending gifts.

"My heart was crushed. I cried not just that day—not just that night—but for many days, even weeks, because I felt those who loved me most had forgotten me. I can remember developing a complex through that experience. As these feelings took root, I convinced myself: 'You can't trust people. Those who say they love you cannot be trusted. They don't really mean it. They don't really love you.' My mind played games with me."

James was really hurting. Here is the time that Satan will try to steal your heart with bitterness. At fourteen, James' mother suddenly allowed him to see the Hales. He was thrilled, and when he saw that they had missed him too, he was very confused as to why they didn't send him gifts or call any longer.

During this period with the Hales, James came to know Jesus. Then James found out the truth about what his mother had done about the presents and the Hales.

"She asked them not to send anymore. Our telephone number was not provided, and for many years we did not even have a phone. My mother would not give them our address, and because we moved so often, it was difficult to track us. I did not understand why she cut us off. My first feelings were anger, bitterness, hostility, and even hatred toward my mother. How could she do something so thoughtless, so heartless?

"But over the next weeks when I returned home, and during the next months, God's grace began to take effect. Suddenly, the true meaning of Scripture—that He became poor so that we through His poverty might be rich—began to find expression in my own heart. No, it was not material wealth. It was not physical riches. Instead, it was an eternal wealth that cannot be bought with gold and silver.

"God's grace worked forgiveness and understanding in my heart. You see, my mother's parents died when she was very young—her mother passed away when she was nine years old and her father died when she was eleven. As a very young girl, she married a man who said he loved her, and yet their marriage did not last.

"Many men had said they loved my mother, but they hurt her and broke her heart. My own father forced himself on her. As a result of being used and abused, my mother lived a very lonely life full of heartache and pain. Now she had a little son—a son she had to give up for a few years after her birth. But then she took him to be with her.

"Starting at age five through age fifteen, she had a little boy who loved his mother! And why wouldn't I? When taken from the security of Mommy and Daddy, she was all I had, and I clung to her as though she were life itself. I trusted her and had confidence in her. And then when I found out what she had done, I was devastated.

"But that indescribable grace working in my heart helped me see why my mother had let me down. She wanted someone to focus their love and attention on her, and when she saw others who had the means to give me nice gifts, she saw the potential for my heart to be pulled away—for me to be drawn toward those with more ability to provide. She did not want me to become distracted or to lose my devotion. She wanted somebody, some man, to love her. To hold her. And that man was her own little boy. I understand, even as a teenager, the great need my mother had for somebody to just love her for who she was—and I did.

"Although I was hurt by what she did, God's gift through His Son enabled me to rise above that experience and pain, and to live a life full of mercy, grace and forgiveness for others. I've been hurt other times in my life, and perhaps some of it I have brought on myself. But again and again, God's grace, through His Son Jesus, has enabled me to forgive and offer mercy to so many who have fallen or failed.

"I have seen God restore people who most of society and the church have given up on, and I have watched the miracle of God's grace in action. It's truly a love gift from God. 'For by grace you have been saved through faith, and that not of yourselves; it is the gift of God' (Ephesians 2:8)."

As with the others who chose forgiveness, James Robison is using his life to help others who are hurting.

There are so many types of offenses, but we all fight the battle to overcome. When we realize that we do not see clearly all the details of life, we understand better how to forgive.

While James could have remained a broken man and relived his hurts with each person he encounters, he instead chooses to use his hurts to understand the suffering of other children. James and Betty Robison have helped millions through their humanitarian outreaches. They are well known for digging water wells in Africa and feeding countless starving people. He has turned what was meant for evil into good for himself and others. He gains great satisfaction and joy in helping others.

He adds, "The first opportunity to see the expression of God's matchless gift in my own life was when I was first able to forgive my mother for the decisions she made, which had such an adverse impact on me while I was a little boy and even in my teen years. But God gave me the grace I needed, and my relationship with my mother was very special until the day she went to be with the Lord. I'm thankful to say she was a Christian. She truly loved the Lord very much and in her own way sought to serve Him.

"Another evidence of God's love and grace working in my heart occurred much later in life when I was reunited with the alcoholic man who had forced himself on my mother. This father I never really knew had hurt me so much. But I was able to forgive him.

"I can remember the scene clearly. My father was sick and intoxicated, and as I walked into his small room, I saw that he had thrown up. The stench was awful. Here was a man, filthy, lying in his own vomit—and he was my own dad. A man who had never once bought me any food, given me any clothes, nor provided one area of care was now lying in a difficult situation due to his own addiction and improper choices.

"As I knelt by this very sick man, I pulled him up against my chest and said, 'Daddy, I don't know you, but I love you.' And I meant it. I prayed with him, I wept over him, and with all my heart I tried to lead him to Christ.

"One of my greatest hopes is that when I get to heaven, I may see him. For you see, he died a few days after I had shared Christ's love with him. He did not respond, but my hope is that before departing, he cried out and said, 'God, be merciful to me, a sinner!' And the merciful God, whom we have come to know through the gift of Jesus that first Christmas, gladly received him, and the angels of heaven rejoiced.

"I hope when I get to heaven I will see a man step out from the crowd and wave his hand, saying, 'Son, look here. Here's your old daddy. I trusted Jesus before I died, and now through His grace, I live forever.' It is this grace that we must not only receive, but just as God shared it through His Son, we must also share it with others."

Yes, that truly is where we will find our happiness and joy for eternity.

Evangelist Diana Radabaugh forgave her alcoholic father, and her reward is definitely eternal.

"While my Dad was fighting in World War II, my Mother was giving birth to me. When he returned, the war began in our home. One of the most vivid memories I have is lying on the bed trying to quiet my two-week-old sister, Linda. At the same time I was holding close to my side, my brother Jim. He was just fourteen months old and sobbing as we listened to the sounds of busting glass and loud violent swearing words. It was our Mother and Dad fighting.

"That was the beginning of a life of poverty, shame

and agony. Dad had become an alcoholic, as his Dad had been and his Dad before him. Welfare hand me down clothes and cardboard soles for my shoes were not uncommon.

"We had moved thirty-six times in sixteen years. People did not take kindly not having their rent paid. Plus, there were five children living in an apartment when they were told there were three children. So we would move.

"I remember I would cry over houses that I liked. One home I became personally attached to at ten years old. I went crying from room to room hugging the walls and telling the house that I loved it and I was sorry we had to move.

"Dad had been very violent with Mom; he put her in the hospital twice with broken ribs. It was not unusual to take her cold cloths for her bleeding mouth. I remember seeing her drinking coffee and smoking cigarettes at the kitchen table. She'd stare out into nothing with tears running down her eyes. Dad had left her again to run around and drink up any money he had.

"I was about twelve years old at my Grandmother's house one day. She greatly loved me and I loved her. There was crying coming from up stairs. Compassion guided my footsteps up the stairs and I slowly opened a nearly shut door. There sitting on the edge of the bed in the middle of the day sat my Dad's mother. She was crying very hard. I quietly slipped up beside her, reached my hand out to touch hers, and said, 'Grandma, what is the matter?' She told me a story that would stay with me for the rest of my life.

"'Diana, I know that it will not be long before I die

and go to heaven with Jesus. I know that I am the only one on this earth that prays for your daddy's salvation. When I die, there will be no one to pray for him and he will go to hell. And heaven will not be the same for me without him there.'

"I said 'Oh Grandma I will pray for him, I will,' she stopped crying.

"Intently she looked deep into my eyes and said, 'Will you Diana, will you promise me that you will?'

"'I promise Grandma, I promise I will.' I assured her.

"At sixty-nine years old, a hardened alcoholic with his fifth wife present in his living room, he repeated a prayer with me. He asked Jesus Christ to forgive him of all of his sins and to come into his heart. A couple months later as his pastor, I baptized him in our pool named, Cedar Creek. Then a couple of months later, he received the baptism of the Holy Spirit.

"A couple weeks short of his seventy-first birthday he went home to meet his Savior face to face. I am sure, standing right behind Jesus stood Daddy's Mama smiling from ear to ear.

"Promise fulfilled. Prayer answered. Dream realized."

Angela is one that knows the horrible crime against the innocent. When she was ten years old, she went to visit her married sister living in another state. There, she was not only molested by her brother-in-law, but her sister held her down while he violated her. What could be harder to rise above emotionally, mentally, and spiritu- ally? Angela found hope and victory in Jesus and now as an adult has forgiven her sister and brother-in-law. Now it is the sister that lives in torment of what she's done. She knows Angela has forgiven her, and it seems to make it even harder for her to forgive herself. Angela's sister will not find healing until she too releases it to Jesus. He is the one that gives us strength to forgive others *and* ourselves. We can't expect to understand it, but if we do what Jesus says, we will live free. It works even if we don't understand it.

In his book *Bruchko*[8], Bruce Olsen tells his own story of being a nineteen-year-old off to South American jungles. He immediately faced disappointment when the ones who supposedly were to meet him never came. His long ordeal of many years is absolutely breathtaking. A suspense movie or drama couldn't be more intense in Hollywood.

Bruce records a time when he was in a hut and natives (a murderous tribe) shot arrows into the hut hoping to kill him. Though he was severely wounded, he did survive. He was tortured mentally and physically. He had been captured by rebel guerillas, but worse than that, he was captured by Motilone Indians. They shot an arrow through his thigh and hauled him off to their camp. He escaped and survived. Over and over he faced death from these various people.

Many times you hear of a missionary going out to help people, and the very people they want to help torture them or kill them. This man was so badly tortured it is a wonder he survived. But his story is so amazing that four presidents of Colombia have become his friends, and he has worked to bring peace to a savage tribe. All this couldn't have been possible without love and a dedication to press forward no matter how much it literally hurt.

People can make a tremendous difference when they put away selfish thinking. The "all about me" syndrome is killing. Bruce Olsen could have gotten bitter at people not receiving him at the airport. He could have said the tribes didn't deserve anything good and could have given up. But he persevered, not blaming God for all his troubles but counting all as gain for the job he would complete.

We never know the future good our actions of today will bring. He has changed for the better that part of Colombia and has been greatly praised in the nations for it. His right choice became many peoples' blessing.

Corey Tin Boon is famous for her forgiveness of the Nazi man that murdered her family. Being able to see him face to face and say she forgave him wasn't natural. It took a faith that was supernaturally grounded in God. But she trusted God fully.

Remember Nate Saint, who was killed by tribesman that he sought to help? One of the other missionaries killed that day with Nate was a married man named Jim Elliot. His wife, Elizabeth, could have become bitter and sought revenge. But instead Elizabeth went back to the same place her husband was killed and showed love to the people. She risked her own life to go back and actually offer them medical assistance. She knew the power of forgiveness.

Nate Saint's own son, Steve, looked into the eyes of his father's killer never knowing he was the one. Steve's mother went back and also worked with the natives, never telling her son.

Then years later the killer was overcome with remorse and confessed to the son who was then grown. The killer handed his spear over to his victim's son knowing for sure he would die just the way he had killed.

But with a great struggle to do what was right, the young man made the right choice. He spared his father's killer and forgave him. He went on to even bring him to the U.S. to live in his household. He has accepted his father's killer as a grandfather to his children.

So amazing was this story that a movie was made about it. How can a boy lose his father and then face the killer, only to embrace him? This is totally unnatural.

Certainly this was no easy task, I assure you. The decision was made in an instant. The right choice was made. This too is unnatural. You see, forgiveness is *not* natural. It takes something very special to do the right thing, especially when your emotions can get the best of you.

No one looks at people with bitterness and praises them. It takes something powerful to overcome those feelings and become a hero to forgive. God is surely more powerful than anything.

Some people have a few things in their life to overcome while others seem to have many. So is the life of one Texas minister. At twenty, she thought she was doing the right thing when she found herself pregnant. It would take many years to forgive herself for that abortion. She managed to continue with life and with regrets.

Then one night she was on a date with someone she knew. He raped her. This time when she found herself pregnant, she did not make the same mistake twice. She gave birth to a beautiful boy and chose to raise her son.

Life moved on. She later married, and to her horror she found that her husband had molested her precious son. Life was filled with hurt for the both of them. Then she married again, but again she would be devastated as she found that her husband had been living with another woman only two miles from her home. She admitted wanting him dead at first. But today this precious woman of God has, with the grace of God, risen to help others.

Now she has experienced freedom through forgiveness. She is free to live and free to be who God wants her to be. She spent much time in the school of "hard knocks." But today she has forgiveness for all those who have hurt her. It wasn't easy, but like everyone else who has experienced it, this minister clings to God and forgiveness.

Freedom is worth it all. Forgiveness is for the victim more than for the offender.

My own neighbor, Karen, was conceived in a date rape. She too had the chance to become bitter but chose to overcome. She and her husband have passed on the gift of life by adopting a son. Now sixteen, James is grateful for the gift of life.

Over and over opportunity presents itself for us to grow in the ability to forgive. Each time we forgive, we become more like Jesus. He forgave supernaturally. It just didn't make any logical sense then, and it still doesn't. It is like gravity. We can't explain why or how it is here, but we have to abide by its rules or we suffer.

If most people were asked to invest ten dollars to get one million dollars, while most would think it crazy, they'd likely be willing to give it a shot because ten dollars isn't much to lose.

There are some people who just don't want to believe

anything. I know I have met them. So my question is *why not give up something worth far less to gain something that is worth far more?* What is unforgiveness really worth to you? You know it has to be worth something if you are holding on to it so tightly. But it's all in your mind. *There is no real value in unforgiveness.*

STEPPING INTO YOUR FREEDOM

Well, now what? You have all this encouragement and think you know what to do, but are you going to do it? If you are not a believer, you will still benefit from acting out the forgiveness. However, your own guilt will still remain.

What is the hesitation to believe Jesus really did die for your sins? Accountability? You're accountable regardless. But with Jesus you're forgiven. If you have not taken that step, I pray that you will break through those lying voices to see for yourself a world of hope for the future, free from guilt.

The Bible tells us to simply come to Him (Jesus) and admit our guilt. Tell Jesus you need a Savior. Ask Him to come into your life, to forgive you, and to give you a *real* life. Then make a commitment to follow Him.

He is faithful to forgive you. He has given us a wonderful instruction book to know exactly how we must act. He loves you dearly. There are letters written to you and me in the Bible. See for yourself what He says about *you*. Join other believers to share that joy and life. Don't listen to the voices that say religion is bad, so you shouldn't go to church. People are the ones that make religion bad. Seek a relationship and not a religion, and you will find what God wants for you.

Find people who demonstrate the truth found in the

Bible. Remember it is when we are alone that we are most vulnerable to the enemy.

You have the gift of an open door to the room where the King of the Universe sits. Do not fear approaching Him if you have received the forgiveness Jesus has for you. Voices may say nothing really happened and you are stupid to believe such myths. I challenge you to prove it to yourself.

No one challenges the writings about Plato and Socrates having been written hundreds of years after they died. They do want to question, however, the validity of writings twenty-five years after the death of Jesus. *Over five hundred people saw Jesus alive again!*

There is a battle raging for your soul. Do not allow evil to win. Take hold of Jesus, step into your freedom, and don't look back. You are so loved that God would rather die than to lose you. Know who you are. You are made in the image of God! Parents love looking at their children and pointing at features that resemble them. God does too.

> For God so loved the world that He gave His only begotten son that whoever believes in Him will not perish but have eternal life.
>
> John 3:16

> That if you confess with your mouth "Jesus is LORD," and believe in your heart that God raised Him from the dead, you will be saved. For it is with your heart that you believe and are justified, and it is with you mouth that you confess and are saved.
>
> Romans 10:9

You will be able to overcome those things that are dragging you down.

> You, dear children, are from God and have overcome them, because the one who is in you is greater than the one who is in the world.
>
> 1 John 4:4

Since we have been forgiven much, we ought to be forgiving too.

> Here's an exercise:
> With paper and pen write your offender/offenders' name.
> With your mouth say:
> "I forgive _____ for _____.
> I release them to you, God, and ask you Jesus to release them too."
> Take this paper and throw it away, along with your unforgiveness.

Speaking of love, "it keeps no record of wrongs" (1 Corinthians 13:5).

———

I remember when my current marriage was horrible in my viewpoint. I went to everyone trying to get help. But no one seemed brave enough to confront my husband. I was miserable. So I began writing every single offense in a journal. Page after page after journal after journal, I was keeping account over the year. I had a library of offenses.

Then Richard and I were reconciled. We built a new house, and as we were preparing to move, I pulled all these journals out. I started reading them, and it all rushed back on me, feelings of hurt and bitterness. I hadn't even remembered some of the things I had written!

Then I heard God say to my heart, "Love keeps no record of wrongs. Get rid of them." Did I really want to hold on to them? Unfortunately I must admit I did. But I realized this was a trap, and I had to choose to do what was right. I loved my husband, and we had forgiven each other. He had not kept my wrongs, and neither did God once I asked for forgiveness.

So I threw them all away. I am walking in the rewards of my obedience. It's a great feeling now!

Pray that God bless your enemy. With God all things are possible. When you begin to pray for your enemy, it may not be easy at first, but you *will* begin to see a transformation in your attitude. Something happens, and you start feeling the heart of God for that person.

Hell is an awful place. I can't even say I would want my worst enemy to go there. Since I already know the great reward in my spirit, mind, and body from forgiveness, I choose not to hold on to *any* offenses. Even when I am hurt deeply, I force myself to do what God wants. Once I get past my flesh, there is a great relief and the reward of knowing I am more than a conqueror.

Deciding to do what is right is just the first action to back up any commitment to God. The real test will come when you are face to face with your offender or simply as the days pass. It may be hard to "feel" forgiveness, but you are not required to "feel" it. Instead you must "do" it. Be kind toward your offender when you meet them face to face. When you think of that person, remind yourself that you have chosen to forgive. If you have accepted Jesus' forgiveness, think on how He sees you now. It may have to be a daily exercise until you reach the point of not picking up unforgiveness again. There will always be something to forgive in our lives. It might simply be the guy who cuts us off or our spouse leaving the toothpaste open. The perfection of forgiving is in the practicing.

Jesus says to take up our cross daily. With that constant awareness of what it cost Jesus to give that freedom to us, it will be much easier passing it on to others.

There is no need to tell anyone else that you forgave. This is to be done secretly. Your praise shouldn't come from people telling you how noble it is that you forgave such a great offense. "Then your father, who sees what is done in secret, will reward you" (Matthew 6:4).

No one likes it when a person brags about what good he has done. Neither does God like boasting. Keep your mouth from speaking offensively during an offense. As your relationship grows with the Lord, you will see more control over your tongue. If you continue to fill your thoughts with the things in God's word—the Bible— you will see that your mouth will reflect that. "Out of the overflow of the heart the mouth speaks" (Matthew 12:24).

We must think before we speak. How many times did I hear that growing up? That is something I personally struggle with. I totally understand when Peter chopped the ear off of the centurion who was taking Jesus. I can't understand Peter's denial of Jesus. Maybe Peter just lived the fear without thinking. I rarely have fear, but I too don't think long enough before I speak. My mind rushes all over the place like a search engine. If something doesn't line up with God's word, I want to eradicate it. Forgiveness isn't the first thing most of us think about.

God is patient and merciful, slow to anger. If He isn't jumping my case for everything, then I should be slower with others too. When I am confronted with my wrongs, I'd like to think I am eager to change because I don't want to stay on the wrong side. Sure, I am like anyone else and don't enjoy being corrected. An attitude of gratefulness is better in these situations. You can't have bitterness if you are grateful. I want to be a better person as each day passes, so I look for those things I can be grateful for each day. Most of all I am grateful for Jesus loving me and forgiving me.

Even Jesus couldn't please everyone, and you won't either. Rest in the knowledge that all is safe in His hands, and it is not for us to control the world. We are commanded to love as Jesus loved. Controlling ourselves and forgiving others will result in living by the power of God's love. We must live what Jesus asks of us if we call ourselves Christians, followers of Christ, and anointed ones.

It is truly possible to live in total forgiveness, though it may be hard. Everyone benefits from others living in forgiveness. A great example was my dear friend. This precious woman was absolutely a shining example of God's love and forgiveness. Pastor Linda Shanks never raised her voice and always had a good word for everyone. Love overflowed from her every moment. She gave her love freely, even to those who tried to ruin her. Yes, she showed love to her enemies and never sought revenge. She didn't even talk badly about them. Goodness and mercy followed her all the days of her life because that is what she left behind for everyone she touched. She lived a life of complete forgiveness. It was amazing to see at her funeral all the lives changed by her life of forgiveness. She is greatly missed because everyone wants to be around someone who freely forgives. Our eyes are opened wide as we see just what her life has contributed. There is nothing that anyone can say about this woman except that she loved God and she loved people without reservation. It *is* possible to forgive through the love of Jesus. What a great way to leave our legacy to be passed on for generations. We are inspired to do good when we see good being done. Why not take that first step to do good—to love through forgiveness?

> Love is patient, love is kind. It does not envy, it does not boast, it is not proud. It is not rude, it is not self-seeking, it is not easily angered, it keeps no record of wrongs. Love does not delight in evil but rejoices with the truth. It always protects, always trusts, always hopes, always preserves.
>
> 1 Corinthians 13:4–7

As time goes on, more discoveries show the truth of the Bible. God does not separate the mind and the body from the soul at this time. There will be a time when they will be separated, but for now they affect each other. What we think does affect our body and soul. What we do with our body affects our mind and soul. Finally all will prosper when our soul prospers.

Without Jesus we are only feeding ourselves artificial substance.

We must move forward in truth if we are to move forward at all. I have prayed for you before you even picked this book up. That prayer is for your total freedom in forgiveness, first in the forgiveness that is through Jesus Christ. He alone can forgive us from our imperfections, called sin. *He alone* is the substitute for the punishment we all deserved.

But *you alone* can choose to take that payment for yourself.

I prayed that you make that decision without reservation. If you already have that payment and are saved through Jesus Christ's forgiveness, I thank God for you. However, even if you are saved, you cannot hold unforgiveness in your heart. If you have unforgiveness now because of an offense, the Bible says, "But if you do not forgive men their sins, your Father will not forgive your sins" (Matthew 6:15).

Pastor Gregory Dickow has actually seen great results from a "wrong thinking fast." He has challenged people to stop thinking destructive thoughts and think the thoughts of God. All kinds of results came pouring in, everything from addictions broken to one woman losing eleven pounds! Amazing, right?

It's said that we only use ten percent of our brains. Maybe we should be actively involved in what goes inside our brains. It belongs to us anyway, so why not take control?

I took a few notes of what Pastor Gregory Dickow pointed out about the ways to take our thoughts captive.

1. Increase the security in what comes into our thoughts. Do not allow ungodly thoughts to come in and stay there. We wouldn't let just anyone come into our airplanes, our buildings, or our homes. Pastor Dickow said, "Righteousness should sit at the door of your thoughts.⁹" Righteousness is your guard! If God wouldn't think those thoughts, then they shouldn't be allowed to get in.

2. Meditate on the word of God day and night (Joshua 8:1). It is not whether you read the Bible all day and night but whether you *think* about God's word all day and night. Reflect and remember what you *do* know in God's word when you are not reading it.

3. Speak God's word aloud. Pastor Gregory demonstrated the power in this with an exercise that you can do also. Start counting silently in your thoughts to ten. Say your name aloud in the middle of counting. Your thoughts are stopped immediately. So when you start thinking wrong thought, *speak* the word of God about your situation. You are more than a conqueror (Romans 8:37), and you have the mind of Christ (2 Corinthians 2:16). This will stop your wrong thoughts telling you not to forgive. Read aloud the reference verses in this book.

It isn't worth your life to hang on to unforgiveness. Let it go—now! Do everything you can to rid yourself of this life threatening disease of unforgiveness.

You can only do that fully through the power of Jesus Christ. If you haven't accepted His payment, His own death and punishment for your sins, I ask you to do so now. The longer you put it off, the harder it will be to come to Christ.

Be patient and apply what you have read to your life. Be consistent. God's truth never fails. God has given you all that you need to succeed. Believe that though forgiveness cannot change the past, it will change your future incredibly.

God bless you.

End Notes

1   End of the Spear Oklahoma City:
     Every Tribe Entertainment, 2007

2   Alfred Lord Tennyson, In Memoriam, 1850, line 27,
     stanza 4
     English poet (1809 - 1892)

3   Washington Irving quotes (American Writer called the
     first American man of letters. Best known for the short stories
     The Legend of Sleepy Hollow and Rip Van Winkle. 1783–1859)

4   Jefferson, Thomas. Letter to messers Nehemiah Dodge,
     Ephraim Robbins, & Stephen S. Nelson a committee of
     the Danbury Baptist association in the state of
     Connecticut. Washington D.C.: Library of Congress, 1802

5   Alexander, Noble with Rizzo, Kay D. I Will Die Free
     Nampa: Pacific Press Publishing Association, 1991.

6   Alexander, Noble with Rizzo Kay D. I Will Die Free
     Nampa: Pacific Press Publishing Association, 1991, p 142

7   Wurmbrand, Richard. Tortured for Christ
     London: Hodder & Stoughton, 2004

8   Olson, Bruce. Bruchko Lake Mary: Creation House, 1995

9   http://fromtheinsideout.us. Dickow, Gregory

Resources

Case for A Creator by Lee Stroebel
Mere Christianity by C.S. Lewis
Focus on the Family's Truth Project Video Series
www.focusonthefamily.com
www.GregoryDickow.org
www.answersingenesis.org

Great books to build your faith:
Bruchko by Bruce Olsen
I Will Die Free by Noble Alexander
Tortured for Christ by Richard Wurmbrand
Battlefield of the Mind by Joyce Meyer

Contact Information

To contact the author, please visit www.juda4praise.com
Prayer requests and/or testimonies of how
this book has helped are welcomed.